ANALYSIS OF CHANGING RURAL WOMEN'S REPRODUCTIVE BEHAVIOUR PATTERNS IN SOUTH AFRICA

Zn Mfono

Organisation for Social Science Research

in Eastern and Southern Africa (OSSREA)

Printed in Ethiopia

ISBN: 978-99944-55-34-8

Organisation for Social Science Research in
Eastern and Southern Africa (OSSREA)
P.O. Box 31971
Addis Ababa, Ethiopia
E-mail: ossrea@ethionet.et
Web site: http//www.ossrea.net

OSSREA acknowledges the support of the Swedish International Development Co-operation Agency (Sida/SAREC), Norwegian Agency for Development Co-operation (NORAD), and The Netherlands' Ministry of Foreign Affairs.

CONTENTS

EXECUTIVE SUMMARY

This report presents a description of the patterns of change in rural women's reproductive behaviour in South Africa over a period of 17 years extending from 1987–9 to 2004. The analyses were informed by the Programme of Action that was set out at the 1994 International Cairo Conference on Population and Development. The Programme of Action has a 20-year implementation time period, and the year 2004 was halfway through the 20 years. The year 2004 is also 30 years since the introduction of South Africa's National Family Planning Programme in 1975, which advanced the health rationale for fertility regulation. It is also twenty years after the introduction of the Population Development Programme in 1985, which emphasized the demographic rationale for fertility regulation. It is finally the seventh year after the introduction of the Choice on Termination of Pregnancy Act in 1997, which legalized pregnancy terminations under prescribed conditions, with emphasis on women's rights to choice.

Guidelines and strategic approaches on provision of reproductive health services that balance women's rights and health considerations with demographic, developmental and poverty alleviation considerations are provided in the Programme of Action. The ultimate aim is bringing about changes in all societies that contribute to the Millennium Development Goals of poverty alleviation and development.

Secondary data from the 1987–89 and 1998 South African Demographic and Health Surveys was analysed, along with reproductive health service records data for 2004, collected from two rural hospitals in each of the three provinces included in the study.

The focus of this research on black rural women emanates from the fact that they constitute a large proportion of reproductive age women, who, for various reasons, are at the rearguard of the reproductive changes that are afoot nationally.

Five of South Africa's nine provinces, which have more than 50 per cent of their populations living in tribal areas, were included in the analyses. The focus of the analyses was on the patterns of childbirth, contraception, voluntary surgical sterilizations and pregnancy terminations. The age and marital patterns of childbearing onset and progression, contraception, voluntary surgical sterilizations, pregnancy terminations, as well as changes in number of children born were analysed across the selected provinces. Comparisons with the national trends and between provinces are made. The observed dynamics were also compared with findings of similar analyses done in other African and in Caribbean societies, and finally with those observed in Asian and European societies. Qualitative findings derived from a 2002 study that employed focus group discussions with rural women were used to determine the significance of the changes from the perspective of rural women, as well as the motivations for women's selective compliance with the various aspects of change.

The findings indicated an upward shift in childbearing ages and a progressive fall in the mean number of births per woman, but both aspects varied according to women's reported marital status. The median age at onset of childbearing shifted modestly from 19 years in 1987–89 and 1998 to 20 years, with considerable delays in the timing of subsequent childbirths, especially the second childbirth, which had a mean spacing reaching a maximum of seven years in 2004. Child spacing was, however, uneven with the mean years between higher order childbirths progressively narrowing. Provincial variations in ages at childbearing onset were modest.

Lower order births had predominance across the periods considered, and growing proportions of childbearing-age rural women had zero childbirth. The proportions of higher order births reflected a progressive decline during the periods compared. These trends accounted for the decline in the mean number of childbirths per woman during the three time periods compared.

Both contraception and pregnancy terminations during the periods considered had predominant use amongst women in the 20–24 years age cohort. Within their brief history, pregnancy terminations shifted from reflecting neither age nor parity patterns in 1998, to a predominant use by younger age cohorts in 2004. Surgical sterilizations, which appealed to women in their 40s in 1987–89, also changed to a predominance of younger age cohorts during the recent time periods, but the modal parity at which rural women request sterilizations has increased in recent years.

Both contraception and pregnancy terminations appeared to play a significant role in child-spacing than in the postponement of childbearing onset. Surgical sterilizations played a much significant role in limiting the number of childbirths amongst married than amongst single women. Accessibility and use of reproductive health services amongst South African rural women appeared to be good, but sub-provincial variations that require attention appeared to be a problem. The demand for pregnancy terminations was apparently high, and rural women relied heavily on referrals to the health centres that provide this service.

Although the distinction between single and married women is difficult to make because marriage tends to be a long drawn process in the African cultural context, women who identified themselves as currently single reflected an earlier onset of childbirths but a lower number of children ever born than currently married women. Due to their larger representation in the 1998 and 2004 samples, single women had a stronger pull on the overall directional trends on childbearing. Their large representation in childbearing reflects the high incidence of non-marital childbearing in the subject population, which arises from the high mean marital age, which is estimated at 29–30 years. This high marital age appears to have limited bearing on childbearing onset for many women, but might be the reason behind the narrower spacing of higher order childbirths.

Despite wide criticism of governmental health service provision to rural populations in South Africa in recent years, the findings of this research gave the impression that women's reproductive health services are accessible enough to provide a variety of choices to rural women of reproductive age. The marginal change in age at onset of childbearing and the apparent decline in contraceptive use between 1998 and 2004 might be indicative of a pervasive normative age of onset of childbearing. The question of the impact of children's grants on childbearing onset within the rural poverty context is debatable. If the grants provide an incentive to childbearing onset, one has to contend with the fact that they appear to lose their incentive edge after the first birth. Both child spacing and termination of childbearing, when considered appropriate, appear to be within reach for rural women. The downward shift in the normative age for voluntary sterilizations might be indicative of a growing acceptance of sterilization amongst rural women that increasingly frees them from childbearing obligations to meaningful participation in various personal and community developmental initiatives. However, the normative parity for requesting sterilization appears to be rising.

Overall, the reproductive behavioural patterns of rural black women are largely set on the same course as those for their urban counterparts. There are, however, some regional lags, particularly in the former rural Transkei districts of the Eastern Cape Province that have to be addressed. Another challenge is the demand for pregnancy terminations, which presently depends heavily on referrals to a few hospitals that provide the service. This causes delays which in turn result in women requesting the service exceeding the legally prescribed durations for pregnancy terminations.

The fertility transition that is taking place in rural South Africa, while similar to the postulated African transition in some respects, differs from the latter largely in that the high incidence of non-marital childbearing introduces an accelerative momentum to the transition phenomenon. Both the marital ages and ages at onset of childbearing are also much lower in the societies that were used in the analysis that generated the postulated African transition thesis. Marital prevalence is also high in the polygamous contexts that were considered as basis for the thesis. The South African rural fertility transition context is, however, characterized by considerable postponement of childbearing onset, even more pervasive child spacing and a growing limiting of use of childbearing through surgical sterilization. There is substantial and apparently conscious regulation of childbearing.

The high incidence of non-marital childbearing amongst South African black women has its parallel in both Botswana and Latin American and Caribbean societies, where its dynamics were subjected to more intensive analyses. The backgrounds of the Asian and European women's reproductive change patterns provide tenuous comparative scenarios because of the cultural distance of childbearing norms.

Focus group discussions conducted with women of different age cohorts indicated that normative patterns of reproductive behaviour have developed, which integrate reproductive health technology into the reproductive traditions. The emerging reproductive patterns are distinctive, and reflect women's optimal choices, taking into account their perceived economic, health, beauty, social and other realities.

From a policy perspective, the role of men as reproductive partners—an issue that came up strongly in the 1994 Programme of Action—still warrants strategic interventions to place men and women on an equal footing on this important aspect of change in their societies. Adolescent disruption of schooling because of pregnancies, despite accessible family planning services, remains a problem. The decline in childbearing amongst South African rural women requires alternative life options for women, whose time only a few years ago was absorbed by producing and nurturing children. Rural women need alternative developmental challenges that can provide new meaning to their lives and benefit their societies.

List of Abbreviations

ARAG	Abortion Reform Action Group
CEB	Children Ever Born
CFD	Commercial Farming Districts
EC	Eastern Cape Province
HDI	Human Development Index
IUD	Intra-Uterine Devices
KZN	KwaZulu-Natal Province
SADHS	South African Demographic and Health Survey
SMAM	Singulate Mean Age at Marriage
TL	Tubal Ligation
TOP	Termination of Pregnancy

ACKNOWLEDGEMENTS

This research was conducted with financial support from OSSREA, which is hereby gratefully acknowledged. Support and encouragement from the University of Fort Hare Management and its Govan Mbeki Research Development Centre is also gratefully acknowledged. The Research Divisions of the Provincial Departments of Health and the Medical Superintendents and hospital staff members of the selected rural hospitals accommodated the data collection for this research in their busy schedules, and are all hereby gratefully acknowledged. My research assistant, Ms Zandile Mnguni, was a dependable partner during my field work and through the different phases of this project. Without the support of all these parties, this project would never have achieved its fruition.

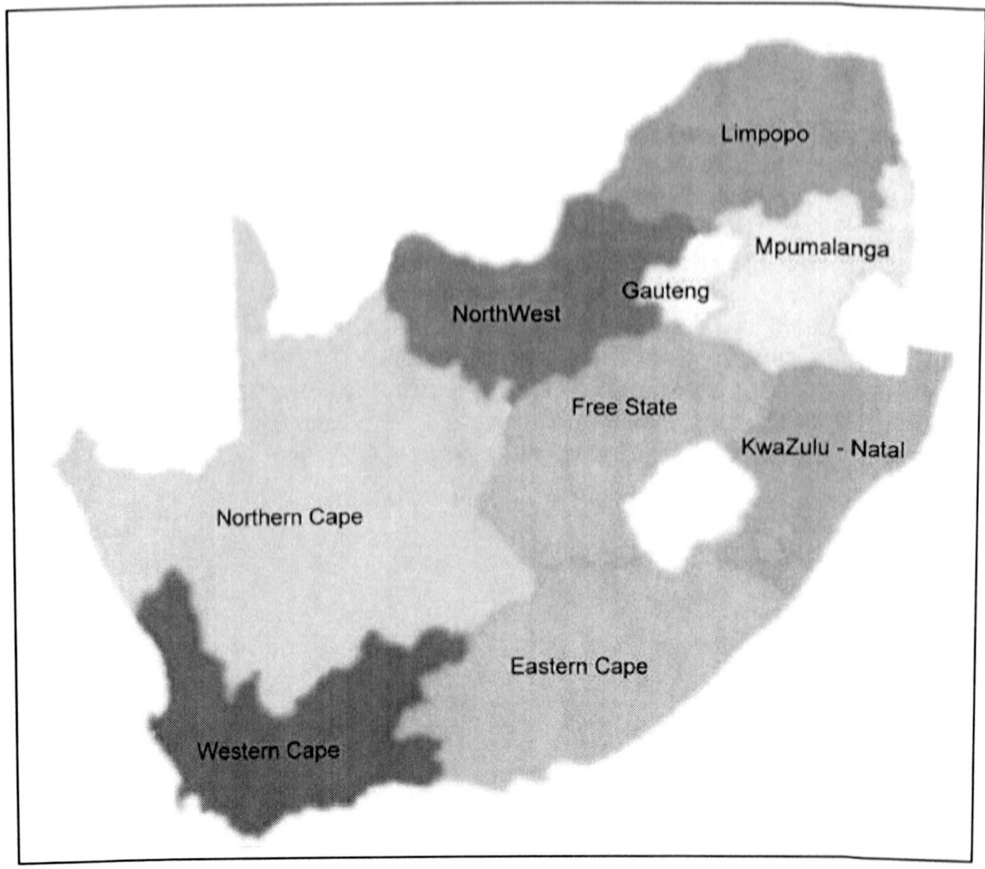

Figure i. Map of South Africa

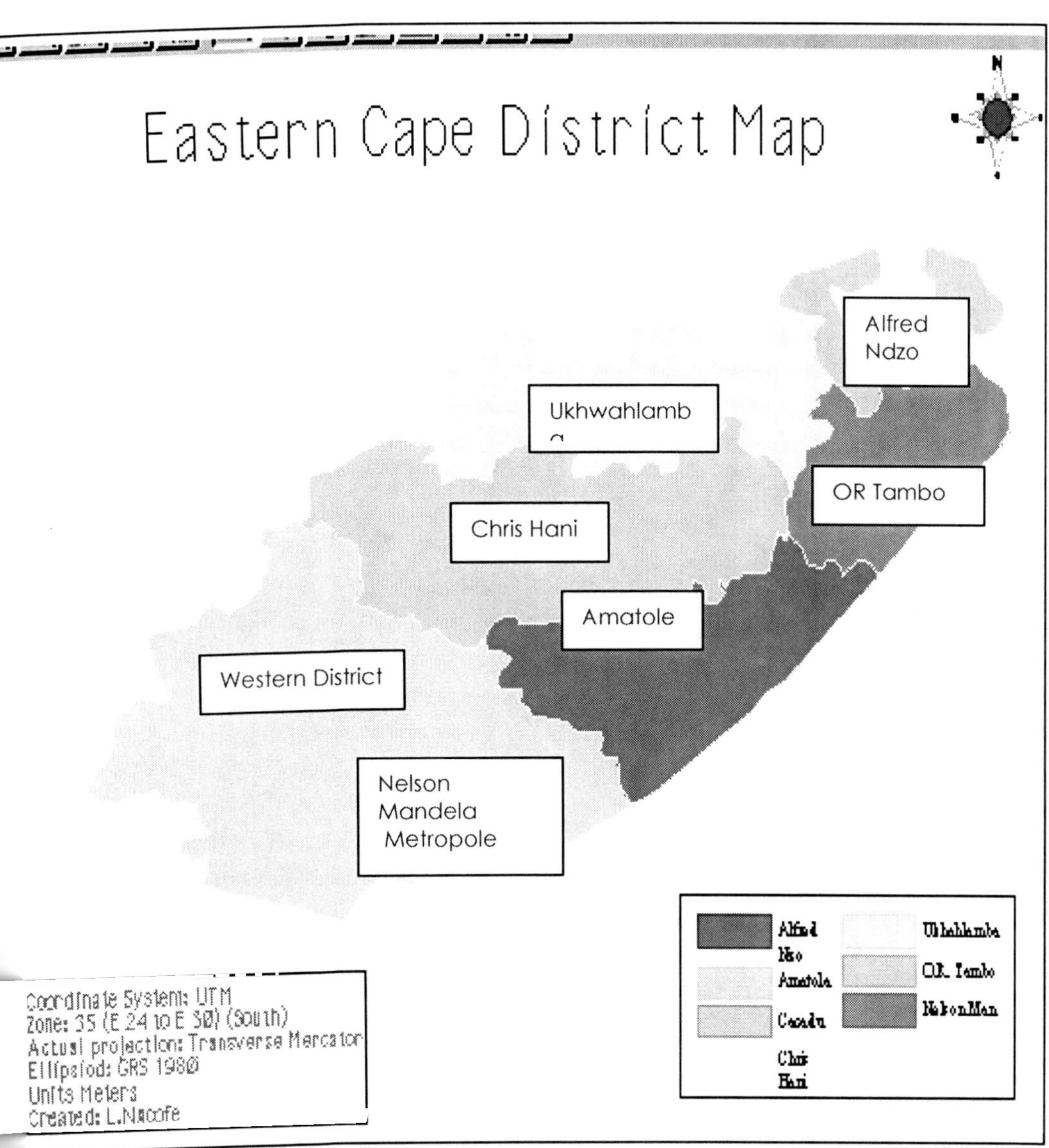

Figure ii. Map of Eastern Cape District

INTRODUCTION

Reproduction is not only an important survival requirement for societies, but changes in its patterns constitute milestones with ripple effects that leave lasting imprints on societies. Since the 18th century AD, world societies have been the scene of much more dynamic changes in reproductive patterns than before, and have subjected such changes to intensive analyses directed at understanding their determinants, pace, dynamics and implications. The "baby boom" and the "baby bust" among western societies after the end of World War II, as well China's fertility decline due to its one-child per family policy attracted worldwide attention because of the scale of the changes they brought about within those societies, and their implications for various aspects of living in the affected societies. Smaller societies also go through similar changes altering their fundamental features and ways of life irrevocably.

Human reproduction also reflects outcomes of changing power relations between the core players, the reproductive couple in the first instance, and between the couples and their families, clan, community and the wider society in which they live in the second instance. However, in recent years, reproduction has also reflected global concerns on population growth, in an era that heightened the use of technological interventions in the regulation of reproductive patterns, and when governments and powerful development institutions that mobilized into a synergy putting an indelible mark on human reproductive patterns. From the Programme of Action set out at the Cairo Conference on Population and Development in 1994, there emerged a strong emphasis on the human rights-based outlook on reproduction that challenges the layers of power relations which marked women's reproductive patterns through history. The Programme of Action located reproductive decision-making on women, recognizing their bodily integrity, health and human rights needs and choices.

This research is basically an evaluative analysis of the practical implementation of the Programme of Action amongst rural women in South Africa ten years after the South African government participated in its formulation and endorsed its principles and strategies.

Many governments endorsed the new outlook to reproductive behaviour, even though some indicated reservations on some of its aspects. This movement has effectively launched a new global outlook on the reproductive role of women. The new outlook challenges women themselves, their spouses, their communities, their societies, and governments to evolve women's reproductive scenarios that incorporate women's personal choices, the health realities that reproduction entails, and the developmental aspirations that women might have for themselves, their progeny and their societies. This new human rights-based rationale for childbearing regulation further views women as basically human and therefore as having rights from which their reproductive choices coupled with a developmental participation agenda must emerge. It can be viewed as one of the pivotal aspects of women's empowerment, and aims at doing away with the traditional central role reproduction has played in shaping women's lives in their societies. It can be regarded as a revolutionary concept which, only a few years ago, was way beyond what could be conjured up since women had no say in the shaping of their reproductive role. Prior to the emergence of this empowering concept, extreme cases included the use of their reproductive capacities to produce slaves cheaply, irrespective of who sired the progeny. The quest for male progeny in many societies also resulted in women having to produce children until the requisite number of male children had been achieved.

The emergence of reproductive technology in the 19th century and its progressive accessibility and acceptance in modern societies has placed a powerful tool into the hands of women to ward off the layers of external control of the reproductive capacity nature endowed them with. Women's reactions to reproductive regulation technology have, however, varied enormously, producing a variety of reproductive scenarios.

The term "reproductive behaviour patterns", as used in this discussion, encompasses actual childbearing, along with various actions women engage in to deliberately mediate its course. Such actions may include sexual abstinence, contraception by various methods, including sterilizations and pregnancy terminations. Such actions may in turn produce distinctive age patterns of onset, progression and termination of childbearing, along with changes in the number of children born to women. "Reproductive patterns" suggests that such actions and their outcomes do not emerge haphazardly but systematically, as products of social environmental factors that impinge on women's behaviour, directing the course of their actions into recognizable outcome patterns.

Analyses of reproductive patterns and the factors underlying them have been integral to inquiries about the unfolding of social phenomena. The analyses of fertility decline in Europe since the eighteenth century (Coale and Watkins 1986) sought to explain the behavioural determinants of changes in women's reproductive patterns during a period that preceded the emergence of modern contraceptive technologies. Family planning technology emerged later, with various methods establishing themselves as effective and efficient tools for regulating women's reproduction. This research focuses on how they impacted on the subject populations of rural women.

The contexts in which reproductive changes occur invariably generate distinctive patterns of change that are outcomes of interactions with local traditions. Women also internalise norms that make it difficult for them to embrace changes that might benefit them and their families, largely because of their powerlessness in the face of social pressures. African societies reflected much slower responses to the reproductive technological changes that generated reproductive changes in the Asian and Latin American developing regions. Within that context, rural patterns of change have even been slower, and analyses of the African rural scenarios suggest that reproductive health programmes in Africa do not adequately reflect the specific socio-cultural characteristics of rural populations. The South African rural context is, however, currently the scene of women's reproductive changes, which require monitoring directed at informing policies and debates that steer them in directions that benefit the affected societies. The United Nations Population Fund (UNFPA) (1997, 102) noted inadequate research on Primary Health Care and reproductive health in South Africa as a shortcoming that creates difficulties in addressing the great geographical, ecological, ethnic and cultural diversities. The continued research focus on the differentials between the four South African racial groups and urban and rural differentials at the expense of comparisons of the various black ethnic groups was also criticized. This research acknowledges the importance of sub-national analyses, and seeks to compare the patterns of change observed among black rural populations of diverse ethnic backgrounds and diverse geographic sub-regions.

Within the context of rural poverty in South Africa, it is important to keep watchful eyes on the trends in the delivery of basic services, including reproductive health services, to rural populations as the Population Policy for South Africa (Department of Welfare 1998) indicates. This is also important from women's social developmental perspective. The focus on black women in this research emanates from recognition of the reality that blacks constitute the numerically predominant group, particularly in the rural areas of South Africa. In addition, changes in the reproductive behaviour of blacks had the most recent onset compared to changes among the other South African groups. This recent onset is occurring at a time when there is expressed governmental interest in women's social and economic advancement. Weaknesses in access for rural reproductive health and outlooks that derogate women's reproductive rights might constrain such advancement.

One of the recommendations of the Programme of Action that emanated from the 1994 Cairo Conference on Population and Development was that governments should elevate women's reproductive health and reproductive rights in their national agendas. It is now more than ten years after the South African government was party to this recommendation, and it is important to evaluate whether any benefits from the Plan of Action are accruing to the most disadvantaged group of women, namely rural women.

South Africa's National Family Planning Programme was introduced in 1975, and in 2004, it had served South African women for 30 years. Although initially based on the health rationale for family planning, the programme may have suffered setbacks during the apartheid years, when the demographic rationale challenged the health rationale within a politically charged environment in which there was no human rights rationale to consider, where the black population was concerned. The survival and growth of the patronage of National Family Planning Programme might probably be attributed to its strong marketing strategies, which drew women's attention to its personal and family benefits beyond the political agendas of the time. This research thus also serves to evaluate the achievements of that programme amongst rural women.

Comparing the pattern of reproductive changes of the research population group with the pattern that has been identified as a distinctively African pattern emanates from a recognition of the common cultural features between the black population of South Africa and the African populations elsewhere in Africa. However, such cultural commonalities may have been attenuated by other factors, and such attenuation may also vary across the regional contexts considered. Polygamy, which keeps reproductive age women in formal reproductive unions, is, for instance, still adhered to in some African societies but has declined considerably in South Africa. But comparable to women in Botswana, the Caribbean and Latin American societies, substantial proportions of black South Africa women reproduce outside formal marital unions. The extent of non-marital childbearing is, however, difficult to determine because marriage in African traditions is not an event but a process that unfolds over time, with reproduction being embedded on the unfolding marital unions.

This research is conducted from the development studies, social demographic and gender disciplinary perspectives. Still, it incorporates strands from the various disciplinary perspectives like economics, anthropology, and sociology that have contributed to an understanding of the phenomenon of reproduction and fertility transition among societies, its determinants and implications. The research combined secondary data from two demographic and health surveys (1987–88 and 1998) with data collected from 2004 reproductive health service records from a sample of rural hospitals. Findings generated from 2002 focus group discussions on the salient aspects of this research were incorporated in the discussion section. That is done to highlight the significance of the observed changes to women, their behavioural motivations and resistances to change on selected aspects, and on non-marital childbearing which constitutes one of the hallmarks of the reproductive changes in the analytic context.

This research set out to analyse and describe the changes in the ages at onset, progression, termination of childbearing, number of children ever born to women of childbearing age, and fertility regulation by different means among rural South African black women over the period of approximately 17 years, extending from 1987–2004. It postulates variations in these changes by marital status and by province, as well as some similarities between the changes and those identified as characterizing the African demographic transition.

Chapter One provides an outline of the theoretical discourses which provide the lens through which women's reproductive patterns and their changes over time can be viewed. It focuses on fertility transition theories, economic theories on fertility changes, the dominant ideology thesis, the self-conscious choices that emanate from critical evaluations of reality and a desire to change it, as well as eclectic theoretical perspectives on reproductive changes. The variables used in this research and their respective contribution to shaping reproductive trends of societies are then sketched out, and the research context is mapped out.

Chapter Two provides a review of literature on the evolution of interactions between reproductive technology and changes in social perceptions of reproductive behaviour in the research context. Literature that highlights the rationales of reproductive technological interventions and western and African societal reactions to such interventions was explored. Then literature providing an exposition of the 1994 Cairo Conference on Population and Development paradigm on recommended governmental interventions on women's reproductive behaviour was focused on.

In Chapter Three, the design of the research and the methodological approaches used at each step in the research process is given, along with the constraints of this research. Chapter Four provides the findings from the analysis of data. Provided in Chapter Five is discussion of the findings and the recommendations.

CHAPTER 1

THE RESEARCH PROBLEM, THEORETICAL UNDERPINNINGS, RESEARCH AIM, AND OBJECTIVES

In this chapter, women's reproductive patterns as subject for social scientific research are presented, along with the theoretical underpinnings of the regulative interventions on them, based on the human rights, the health and the demographic perspectives. An exposition of the evolution of these perspectives and their interactions with economic theories and other dominant ideologies and power dynamics is given. A postulation of the impact of the unfolding of democracy on rural women's reproductive patterns and the attendant regulative patterns in the research context was also made. Next the variables used in analyses of reproductive behaviour were explored in detail, and their relevance to the present study was evaluated. Finally, the socio-demographic, economic and other salient attributes of the subject populations were explored.

1.1 Some Theories with Relevance to Women's Reproductive Patterns

Prior to the 1994 Population and Development Conference that was held in Cairo, analyses of women's reproductive behaviour were largely subsumed under the broad phenomenon of demographic transition, which was described by Notestein (1953). This was because of the dominance of the demographic perspective on reproductive behaviour outlooks. The concerns about the size and growth of national populations that date back from ancient societies were fuelled by the 19th century Malthusian theories, and research on approaches and achievements in the regulation of childbearing, and the theories produced remarkable outcomes. However, many proponents of fertility regulation by means of scientific methods were dissatisfied with that turn of events. As Gordon (1977) noted, regulation of childbirth by means of modern methods historically unfolded initially around the human rights rationale, which posited that women should be enabled to regulate childbearing. Even though it could be argued that the rights of women were submerged in the rights of their spouses, world societies endorsed the rights of couples to family planning as far back as the 1968 Conference that was held in Teheran (United Nations 1968). The health rationale emerged next, and emphasized the health benefits of reproductive regulation both for women and their offspring. The World Health Organization in its Alma Ata Declaration (1978) also highlighted maternal and child health care, including family planning in its primary health care promotion agenda.

The demographic rationale which viewed unregulated childbearing as leading to overpopulation and various negative outcomes was the last to emerge. Despite its late emergence, the demographic rationale captured the imagination of many influential individuals and institutions, and time saw a gradual relegation of the other rationales to the background, with the growing anxiety about world population growth. The theoretical achievements of the demographic rationale of analyses of women's reproductive patterns have indeed been vast. It is important to acknowledge that the relevance of the demographic analytic rationale to fertility regulation was never challenged. It is the extremist position that posited a deterministic link between high fertility and poverty, along with the practical approaches to fertility regulation from a demographic perspective that generated revulsion. That was because of its alleged disregard for human rights, and sometimes of women's health imperatives. Otherwise, many social scientists, especially economists, reacted positively to the demographic rationale for fertility regulation and developed theoretical perspectives that are linked to it.

It took the Programme of Action that was mooted at the 1994 Population and Development Conference to restore the human rights and the health rationales for regulating childbirths to a respectable position in discourses and governmental action agendas in support of women's reproductive behaviour. From an analytic perspective, this new paradigm, while not discrediting the demographic outlook on women's reproductive regulation, emphasizes the synergy that must emanate from a combination of the three rationales in addressing the contemporary human rights and developmental concerns.

Feminist thinkers provided the driving force for the human rights and health rationales, which have eventually gained a firm footing, with world societies being progressively attuned to incorporate human rights as one of their primary considerations of social phenomena. Hooks (1981, 74) noted that the inability of women in modern society to gain control over their bodies in regard to childbirth was a primary impetus behind the women's liberation movement. Commenting on the scenario in the USA, she noted that lower class women and consequently many black women had the least control over their bodies, while middle class women, for instance, commanded resources that enabled them to terminate unwanted pregnancies. Women with lower educational and income achievements in many societies face similar disadvantages.

1.1.1 *The Demographic Theoretical Formulations of Child-Bearing Regulation*

A demographic transition is constituted by a decline in the incidence of childbirths and deaths over time. Fertility transition, which is the progressive change of individual societies from higher to lower birth rates, has been subjected to global, regional and national surveys of women's reproductive attitudes and behaviour such as the World Fertility Surveys (United Nations 1987), the various Contraceptive Prevalence Surveys and the Demographic and Health Surveys. Findings from such analyses generated formulations of a universal theoretical framework into which the various reproductive behavioural patterns can fit. The journey along this path remains incomplete, and micro-analyses like the present one contribute a step to it.

Notenstein (1953) postulated that in order to survive, peasant traditional societies throughout the world brought pressure on their members to reproduce themselves, to offset high mortality. Such pressure, he argued, was strongly supported by popular beliefs, formalized in religious doctrine, and was enforced by community sanction. According to this view, the defining milestone for transition to lower childbirths among societies was the emergence of parity-specific fertility limitation. That entailed the modification of reproductive behaviour by couples to avoid having more children, after the maximum desired number of children were born. Such limitation marked the movement of societies from reproductive patterns characterized by natural limitation of childbearing to parity-specific limitation or deliberate and purposeful limitation. It is the playing out of these dynamics at the micro-level that is the subject of this research.

Henry (1961) introduced the distinction between natural limitation of childbirths and parity-specific limitation, arguing that the various forms of behaviour that reduce the chances of conception, without being directly intended to have that effect, constitute non-parity-specific or natural limitation. Post-partum sexual abstinence and periodic separation of spouses that reduce their sexual activity constitute natural limitation of childbearing. Breast-feeding on the other hand is known to reduce conception, and is sometimes consciously used to delay it, even though its primary purpose is infant nourishment. Late marriage in contexts in which pre-marital sexual activity is minimal constitutes a powerful method of natural limitation of childbearing.

In its practical application to various societies, the demographic rationale to fertility regulation tended to divorce reproductive control from the individual's conscious choice and personal benefits, replacing these with national and international population goals that lay beyond the comprehension and immediate interests of users of the method. These tendencies opened the demographic rationale to criticism of being oppressive. Freire's (1993) description of attempts to liberate oppressed people without their reflective participation in the act of liberation applies well to this context. He views such treatment as treating people as objects, and describes the manipulative use of technological advances in such contexts as follows, "More and more, the oppressors are using science and technology as unquestionably powerful instruments for their purpose: the maintenance of the oppressive order through manipulation and repression. The oppressed, as objects, as "things" have no purposes except those their oppressors prescribe for them" (Freire 1993, 42).

However, while Freire is vocal about governmental oppressors that manipulate subject people through oppressive educational approaches and content, his thesis has no reference to cultural traditions that submerge the subjective consciousness of individuals, in this context, women. Guy

(1990) describes how in Southern Africa's pre-capitalistic societies, importance was given to the creation of labour power through reproduction. He adds that control and appropriation of both the productive and reproductive capacity of women was central to the structure of these societies. Women, their offspring and cattle indicated wealth, and the societies were based on the accumulation of people as distinguished from societies in which wealth is based upon the accumulation of things. In Guy's view, pre-capitalist societies can be seen as having come to an end with the introduction of social structures based on the accumulation of commodities.

However, even in the context described earlier, fertility regulation from a demographic perspective was not a foreign concept. Guy (1990) records that during the 19th century in the case of the Zulu political system in Southern Africa, the king exercised direct control over the fertility of his subjects through control and separation of age sets or regiments that were not allowed to marry until the king gave permission. In the Zulu kingdom, Guy goes on to argue, it was not so much the sexual activity but fertility that was controlled. This pattern conformed to the natural limiting of childbirths described by Henry (1961).

Foucault's view (1978, 25) recounts how the emergence of the demographic rationale for regulation of childbirths interfaced with sexual behaviour amongst western societies. He notes that with the emergence of population as an economic and political problem in the 18th century, considerations of population as wealth, as human power, as labour capacity, as balanced between its own growth and the resources it commanded were pitched against each other. Governments perceived that they were not dealing simply with subjects, or even with a "people," but with a "population," with its specific phenomena and its variables: birth and death rates, life expectancy, fertility, state of health, frequency of illnesses, patterns of diet and habitation. Foucault, however, acknowledges that the heart of the economic and political problem of population was sex, and analyses were directed at birth rates, the age of marriage, the legitimate and illegitimate births, the precocity and frequency of sexual relations, the ways of making sexual relation fertile or sterile, the effects of unmarried life or of the prohibitions, the impact of contraceptive practices, as well as those of those notorious "deadly secrets" which demographers on the eve of the revolution (of change) knew were already familiar to the inhabitants of the countryside.

The theoretical debates based on the demographic rationale differed in significant ways from those based on the health and human rights rationale, which focused mostly on the woman and her interests as an individual. These will now be explored in more detail.

1.1.2 The Human Rights and Health Theoretical Perspectives on the Regulation of Childbirth

Foucault (1978, 37) commented on what he described as the hysterization view of women's bodies in western societies, up to the end of the 18th century, which is the view of women's bodies that was considered as intrinsically confining women to the reproductive function. He also noted a medical socialization of women, carried out by attributing a pathogenic value to birth control practices. These are some of the social factors the human rights and health outlooks on the regulation of childbirth had to confront.

According to Gordon (1977), during its emergence in the late nineteenth century, scientific family planning was attended by extensive public debates and controversy, and the dominant rationale in its favour was formulated by Heywood in human rights terms as "woman's natural right to ownership and control over her body-self, a right inseparable from woman's intelligent existence"(Gordon 1977, 104).

From a human rights perspective, Gordon explains fertility regulation does not mean population control or birth rate reduction or even planned families, but reproductive freedom, and is part of a larger programme of social change towards a re-discovery of women's humanity in the struggle for total equality. She further explains that from the reproductive rights perspective, involuntary childbearing has burdened all women, particularly poor women, while perpetuating sexual inequality and weakening struggles against it. Reproductive self-determination is considered as a basic condition for sexual equality for women to assume full membership in all other human groups.

The human rights rationale also has a jaundiced view of assertions often expounded from the demographic perspective that high birth rates result in poverty, and views the real issue as the imposition on women of a subordination to reproductive functions that are neither natural nor eternal. According to this view, reproductive freedom is an indispensable element of women's total freedom.

The health rationale for regulation of childbirth emerged from extended debates of the human rights rationale. Stanton cited in Gordon (1977), for instance, challenged the arguments that prescribed compulsory maternity for women as their duty to society—thus: "must the heyday of existence be wholly devoted to the one animal function of bearing children? Shall there be no limit to this but woman's capacity to endure the fearful strain of her life?" (Gordon 1977, 104).

The health and human rights rationales however failed to capture the imagination of the economic theorists as the demographic rationale did. This discussion now turns to how economic theorizing on childbearing patterns evolved over time.

1.1.3   The Economic Theoretical Formulations of Childbearing Regulation

Parity-specific limitation of childbearing typically involves contraception, whether by traditional or modern methods. Economists directly link parity-specific limitation of childbearing to the demand and supply of children. Demand theorists argue that the changing balance between the costs and benefits of childbearing result in a reduced parental demand for children and are the fundamental force behind fertility decline.

The extension of the economic theoretical framework of analysis to childbearing behaviour was introduced by Mill (1909, 1929) in his arguments on the standard of living. He noted that when workers get accustomed to a higher standard of living, they might practice forethought and restraint in their childbearing to preserve that standard. Donaldson (1991) noted that the standard of living argument was prominent among American demographers from the 1880s until the mid-1940s, when it was subsumed under the fertility transition theory. The standard of living argument posits that when the level of wages rises, the standard of living is raised for a time period sufficiently long for people to be accustomed to it. They redefine the quantity of goods and services necessary for a satisfactory mode of living and modify their reproductive behaviour to preserve that standard. Childbearing is adjusted to maintain the progressive standard of living that increases over successive generations and becomes normative.

Cleland and Wilson (1987) argue that the demand theory approach to fertility developed as a branch of the theory of consumer choice and note how the theories of inter-generational wealth flows (Caldwell 1982; Caldwell and Caldwell 1987) combine economic and sociological explanations of changes in reproductive patterns. The theories referred to came from observations of African societies, and indicated that pre-transition societies are characterized by net flows of wealth from children to the older generation. Modernization was observed to cause a reversal of wealth flows, resulting in children becoming liabilities. This prompted a reduction in number of childbirths. Thus Caldwell (1982) argued that childbirth declines rapidly when the moral economy of parent-child relationships places an emphasis on what parents owe children, rather than on what children owe parents.

Handwerker's (1989) theory on the empowering effect of women's access to economic participation also aligns itself with the economic determination of reproductive changes. The findings of his research that was conducted in Barbados indicated that women's dependence on male incomes in the 1950s prompted childbearing that legitimized women's access to men's incomes. Childbearing also ensured that women had adult children to generate income for them. When the scenario changed, and women had direct access to income earning opportunities because of expanded employment opportunities, women's dependence on men's incomes declined dramatically. Children became a consumption rather than the investment item they were to women with no income opportunities. Handwerker uses these economic arguments to explain the decline of fertility in Barbados between the 1950s and the 1980s.

The theories discussed previously each advanced one factor as the rationale for the regulation of childbearing. The theory posited by Bongaarts (1983) discussed next is eclectic because it views childbearing changes as determined by interactions between various factors.

1.1.4 Eclectic Theorizing on Regulation of Childbearing

Eclectic theorizing on childbearing behaviour postulates a combination of economic, psychological and social factors as joint determinants of fertility regulation behaviour. Bongaarts (1983) viewed reductions in childbirth as a product of interactions between various indirect factors like culture, education and economic factors on the one hand and direct determinants which he classified into three groups on the other. Firstly he posits exposure factors such as the proportion of women in marital unions. Next is deliberate marital childbirth regulation by contraception or induced abortion. Finally, there is natural marital childbirth regulation such as extended breastfeeding, intercourse frequency, spontaneous abortion and infertility.

From the studies of the European fertility transition, Coale (1986) suggested three pre-conditions for decline in marital childbearing. Firstly, childbearing must be considered to be within the individual's conscious choice. Secondly, effective techniques for regulating childbearing must be known and available, and thirdly, fertility reduction must be seen as advantageous. Both Bongaarts (1983) and Coale (1986) confine the conditions for fertility change to marital contexts. However, there appears to be no reason against the conditions they postulate being used in evaluating situations of all women in various contexts of exposure to conception.

Coale's reference to conscious choice echoes Freire's "critical reflection", which comes from the emergence of a full humanity that is triggered by educational interventions that help people to "perceive their state not as fated and unalterable, but merely as limiting—and therefore challenging" (Freire 1993, 66).

Rural-urban differentials in reproductive changes are a frequently observed pattern of reproductive changes, in which urban women reflect more accelerated changes than their rural counterparts, although there have been notable exceptions to this observation. The South African change scenario fits in with the commonly observed patterns in this regard. The 1998 South African Demographic and Health Survey found differences between rural and urban women's reproductive patterns in aspects like total fertility, incidence of births to adolescents, contraceptive prevalence and others. But like all social behaviour, changes in women's reproductive behaviour defy rigid theories, requiring them to be applied with qualification. Thus the findings on the analyses of fertility decline in Europe (Knodel and van De Walle 1986) indicated a number of factors that are traditionally theoretically linked with changes in the reproductive behaviour of women but are not necessary for the changes to occur. These factors include rural-urban residence, decline in infant mortality, women's education, and economic development. European societies had varying achievements on these factors when reductions in childbirth occurred.

Questions of the relevance of theories based on analyses of changes in the reproductive patterns of women in western societies to women in the cultural contexts of developing countries have yet to be raised. In other words, how universal are the theories postulated above? It is worth noting that historical fertility analyses revealed differences between the pre-transition childbearing patterns of European societies and those of Asian and African societies. Knodel and van De Walle (1986) describe the pattern of nuptiality that prevailed in pre-industrial Europe as uniquely characterized by relatively late ages at marriage and high proportions of the population remaining permanently single. Coale (1986) estimates that this pattern reduced childbirths by up to 50 per cent of their potential level, if all women of ages 15–50 years were married. This marital pattern contributed to the moderate levels of childbearing in Europe even before the onset of the decline in fertility. Coale, therefore, concludes that entry into and exit from marriage is one of the strategies some pre-industrial societies used to shield a large fraction of potentially fertile women from the risk of bearing children.

In contrast, in the Asian and African pre-transition societies, marriage for women remained early, universal and was prompted by pro-natalist outlooks. In the recent scenarios, where the incidence of marriage has declined, as is the case in the Southern African and some Latin American and Caribbean societies, reproduction that occurs outside formal unions reduces the impact of the low incidence of marriage on childbearing incidence. A further consideration regarding sexual and reproductive norms is the fact that Western and Asian religions considered celibacy and incontinence as virtuous. Thus, Malthus (1992) could appeal for "moral restraint" in sexual behaviour, in the face of population growth. Foucault (1978) pointed to an economic socialization of procreative behaviour and described western sexuality as repressed for economic reasons. Foucault also described a hyper-repressive desublimation, in which sex relied on multiple-channelling into the controlled circuits of the economy. Conversely, to the situation in western and Asian societies, celibacy and incontinence do not appear to have ever enjoyed equivalent levels of respect in African reproductive value systems until the advent of western religious systems. Consequently, the restraint they call for is readily abandoned as a foreign and unnatural imposition.

1.1.5 The Dominant Ideology Thesis in Women's Reproductive Patterns

Western acculturation plays a significant role in various aspects of change in developing societies. Abercrombie, Hill and Turner 1984, 7) cite the views of Marx and Engels that the ideas of the ruling class are in every epoch the ruling ideas, and that the class which has the means of material production at its disposal is at the same time the ruling intellectual force of that society. This argument suggests that the ruling class controls the mental outlook of each society, producing the dominant ideology that submerges the culture of the subordinate classes. "The dominant ideology penetrates and infects the consciousness of the working class, because the working class comes to see and experience reality through the conceptual categories of the dominant class" (Abercrombie, Hill and Turner 1984, 2).

According to this view, while there may be a variety of cultures alongside the dominant culture, in the worst case scenario, all classes are incorporated within the intellectual universe of the ruling class ideas. In their interpretation of the dominant ideology thesis, Abercrombie, Hill and Turner suggest that the dominant class works towards an acceptance and legitimizing of modern society. However, gender analyses often use Marxist theory as a lens for understanding the oppression of women as a class by a male patriarchy dominant force. In that context, patriarchy is viewed as using tradition as the oppressive tool, resisting change and modernization. This is the pressure that was supported by popular beliefs, formalized in religious doctrine and was enforced by community sanction which Notestein (1953) referred to, which submerged the choices of reproductive individuals, particularly those of women. Freire (1993) also makes reference to pressure from a dominant class that supersedes the patriarchal regressive ideological mode from women's reproductive perspective. The reproductive arena is thus depicted as a domain of competing pressures, with each one vying for control.

The advancing western acculturation of the black South African and other developing societies may be weakening the relevance of the caution imposed by the existence of cultural differences, a scenario that suggests submersion of the subordinate cultures. What becomes more pertinent, particularly in the South African reproductive behavioural context are the reproductive behavioural patterns produced by such acculturation, which appear to be dissimilar in many respects both from the Western, as well as from the traditional African reproductive traditions.

1.1.6 Women's Reproductive Changes from the Freirerian Pedagogical Perspective

Freire's theoretical exposition (1993) describes how interventions from a democratic perspective that is sympathetic to the views and interests of oppressed people can produce contrasting outcomes to those from oppressive regimes that have their own agendas. This exposition is also of theoretical relevance to the context of women's reproductive changes considered in this research. Freire argues that in order to struggle for change, people must see their situation not as a closed world with no exit, but as a limiting situation which they can transform. Traditional patriarchy presented women's reproductive patterns with a closed situation. While the demographic rationale for family planning that replaced traditional patriarchal reproductive norms had some redeeming features, in Freirerian terms, it was an instrument of dehumanization, because it attempted to liberate the oppressed without their reflective participation in the act of liberation. For the oppressed to act on their situation, Freire insists, they need to reflect critically on it and engage it creatively.

The Plan of Action that was mooted at the 1994 Cairo Conference on Population and Development opens the way for a meaningful engagement of the realities of the reproductive scenario of women worldwide in ways that might help them take control of their reproductive lives. In the South African context, it can be assumed that the reproductive scenario that is now open to women has been cleared of dehumanizing conditions, both from a gender and from a racial perspective. The period under analysis in this research, therefore, covers contrasting scenarios in terms of the tone of governmental interventions to influence the patterns of women's reproductive behaviour. Patriarchal dominance agendas for women's reproductive behaviour were superseded and overlaid by racially dominant agendas. Theoretically, democracy ushers in the point at which these power forces must yield the way to the needs of women as they perceive them. This is the challenge governments set for themselves at the 1994 Cairo Conference.

1.2 The Research Problem, Objectives, and Aims

1.2.1 The Research Problem

This research set out to describe and analyze the salient aspects of rural women's reproductive behaviour in South Africa as they emerge within a context of social change. The research also sought to identify a theoretical framework that explains these patterns. The behavioural variables focused on were the ages at onset of childbearing, progression to subsequent births and to termination of childbearing, the number of children born to women of reproductive ages, the patterns of regulation of childbirth by contraception, sterilization, and pregnancy terminations, the marital patterns of childbearing and its regulation, as well as the provincial variations in these dynamics. Using secondary data, the research constructs longitudinal pictures of the changes on the aspects considered from 1987–89 to 2004.

South African research on fertility dynamics traditionally focused on quantifying reproductive changes nationally and by the racial categories of the population. In contrast to analyses in Latin American and Caribbean societies, non-marital childbearing which is one of the hallmarks of childbearing amongst black women receives minimal attention. Sub-national analyses, particularly longitudinal analyses of reproductive behaviour change are also uncommon. In addressing these research gaps, this research focuses on rural black populations as an aggregate group and as distinct provincial groups.

The research is conducted during a period of rapid fertility change in South Africa in general, and amongst the black population in particular. The virulence of the AIDS pandemic introduces a dimension that cannot be ignored in analyses of reproductive behaviour. AIDS challenges the sexual norms underlying reproductive behaviour, along with the resistance to sexual abstinence and condom use, both of which must ultimately emerge as significant contributors to changes in the reproductive behaviour patterns considered and their reproductive outcomes. The research incorporates data for up to 10 years after the 1994 Plan of Action formulated at the Conference on Population and Development, and must determine the reproductive health achievements that have accrued to rural women during the intervening period and point to accessibility of the requisite services to rural women. Finally, in 2004, South Africa had its Family Planning Programme serving South African women for 30 years. This analysis thus encompassed an evaluation of how the programme has established itself in the reproductive lives of rural black women, who have remained at the rearmost of the changes in women's reproductive behaviour in South Africa.

1.2.2   The Research Objectives

This research aimed at describing and analyzing the pattern of changes in the reproductive behaviour of rural women, focusing on how the age and marital dynamics of childbearing onset, progression and regulation of childbirths by various measures are changing. Such changes were viewed as indicating reproductive health accessibility to rural women as well as how rural women respond to such services. The time span for analysis was 17 years, extending from 1987–89 to 2004.

1.2.3   The Aims of the Research

The analysis aimed at determining the variations in age patterns, direction, and intensity of changes in the childbearing dynamics and fertility regulation among rural black women in the Eastern Cape, KwaZulu-Natal, Limpopo, Mpumalanga and the North West provinces, using secondary data. The variables used in the analysis were:

i.   Median age of childbearing women at onset of childbearing and at each subsequent birth during the consecutive periods of the research;

ii.   Mean number of children ever born to women of childbearing age at each of the designated time periods;

iii. Mean age, marital status and mean number of previous childbirths amongst women who used contraception, sterilizations, and pregnancy terminations during the designated time periods;

iv. The differences in the childbearing and its regulation patterns by married and unmarried women over the time periods considered;

v. Variations in the changes considered across rural women in the different provinces; and

vi. Parallels in the dynamics observed with African pattern of transition.

The specific questions that the research attempted to generate answers to were: What is the direction and pace of changes in the variables? Do the changes concur with the identified "African pattern" of fertility transition? The research also stratified child-bearing age women into five-year age cohorts as under 20, 20–24, 25–29, 30–34, 35–39, 40–44 and 45–49 years, to determine the changes the selected variables showed for each age cohort over the period considered in the research. The question addressed by cohort analysis is: What recognizable cohort dynamics do the changes reflect?

1.3 The Research Context

1.3.1 Demographic and Other Salient Features of the Study Populations

Table 1.1 Profile of rural black population of South Africa, 1980–2001

Features	Years		
	1980*	1990*	2001**
Males (No.)	7 124 159	9 950 469	8 546 118
Females (No.)	7 348 957	10 413 745	9 889 289
Total (No.)	14 473 116	20 364 214	18 434 407
Average 10-year annual growth (%)		3.23	-.9
Sex ratio (%)	.97	.96	.86
Black population nationally (%)	67	68	52
Total national population (%)	48	52	41

SOURCES: *Development Bank of Southern Africa (1994) **Census (2001)

Except for a small minority that lives in commercial farming districts, South African rural blacks predominantly live in what the 2001 census described as tribal areas. Of the nine provinces into which South Africa has been demarcated since the 1994 democratic political dispensation, the provinces that have large tribal area populations are the Limpopo, North-West, KwaZulu-Natal, Eastern Cape, Mpumalanga. The Free State population living in tribal areas is small, and along with the commercial farming district populations is excluded from this research. The salient features of the rural populations of South Africa are summarized in Table 1.1.

The black population living in tribal areas and commercial farming districts has declined from approximately 48 per cent of the total population of South Africa to approximately 41 per cent over a period of 20 years. This suggests a modest pace of urbanization that is probably offset by the rate of natural growth of the rural population, as suggested by the over three per cent increase of the population between 1980 and 1990. The low sex ratios of this population are associated with male labour out-migration and a high male mortality. The population pyramid of the research population is presented in Figure 1.1.

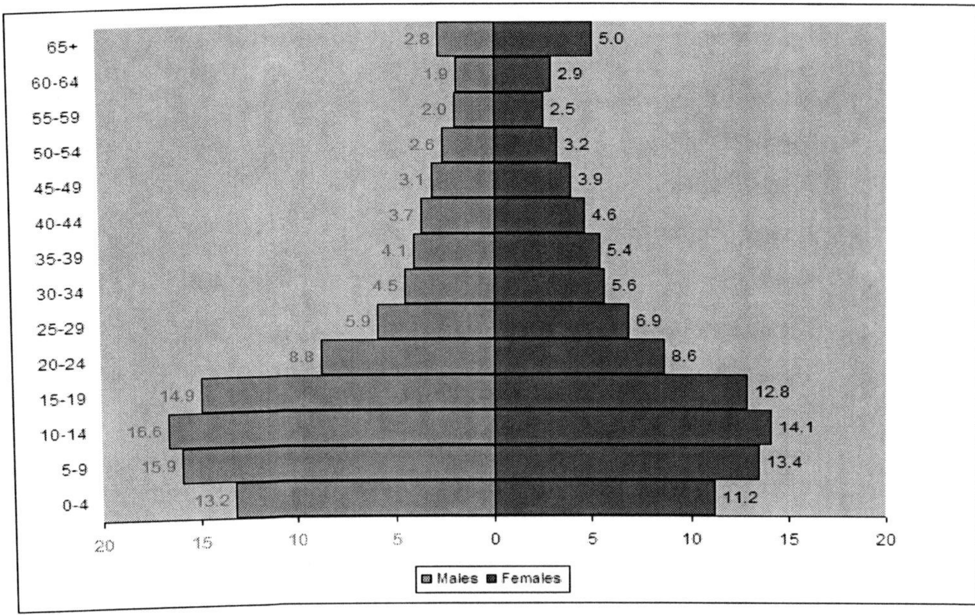

Figure 1.1 Distribution of the Black South African Population in Rural Tribal Areas

SOURCE: Statistics South Africa (2001)

The 2001 rural population of the tribal areas in Figure 1.1, while reflecting a large proportion of young people also has a narrowing base that was afoot for at least 10 years in 2001. This indicates the duration of a fertility decline onset. The deficit of working age adults, particularly males, reflects the shortage of employment opportunities and consequent out-migration of working age adults to urban areas. However, there has also been evidence of a high incidence of widowhood amongst blacks living in the rural areas of South Africa (Statistics South Africa 2002). From a reproductive perspective, this demographic scenario suggests considerable separations of spouses and a compromising of the integrity of household membership. The population over 65 years of age is also large, suggesting that rural areas are viewed favourably for retirement, but also that grand-parents play a significant role as parental surrogates in the absence of parents.

Women's educational achievement is considered an important element of reproductive patterns. Estimates of the historical evolution of rural women's educational achievement in mean years are provided in Table 1.2, and more recent figures on women's educational achievement that came from the 2001 census are presented in Table 1.3.

Table 1.2 The mean years of education amongst rural women, by province

Area	1987–89	1998
South Africa	6.2	8.5
Rural women	5.7	7.4
Eastern Cape	5.9	7.3
Limpopo	6.2	6.4
KwaZulu-Natal	5	6.2
Mpumalanga	5	7.4
North-West	5.7	7.7

SOURCES: HSRC (1987–89), SADH (1998)

The modal years of education achieved amongst women aged 15–49 years in 2001 was 12 years, which is equivalent to Standard 10 in the South African education system. However, as Table 1.3 reflects, the percentages of women in the 15–49 year age category who had no schooling are larger amongst rural women than the percentage of women who completed 12 years of school attendance.

Table 1.3 Educational achievement amongst rural reproductive age women, by provinces

Provinces	Educational achievement of women	
	Women with Std. 10 (%)	Women with no schooling (%)
All South Africa	21	11
All rural black women	12	20
Eastern Cape	13	15
KwaZulu-Natal	17	17
Limpopo	14	20
Mpumalanga	16	18
North-West	18	13

SOURCE: Statistics South Africa (2001)

Rural poverty is a major concern in South Africa where the black population is concerned. Agriculture has a very small contribution to household incomes in the tribal areas, and over the years, there has been a growing dependence on formal sector employment. The 1998 Rural Household Survey indicated that only four per cent of rural household incomes came from agriculture. The declining formal sector employment in recent years results in high rural unemployment, dependence on social transfers and the informal sector.

1.3.2 The Socio-Historical and Economic Landmarks of the Emerging Reproductive Context

Like all aspects of life in South Africa, rural settlement was politically regulated for many years. The 1950 Group Areas Act determined which areas were settled by black populations, and tribal authorities received governmental political, administrative and financial supports. The Group Areas Act also regulated migration of the rural population to urban areas in accordance with the labour requirements of the modern economic sector. This requirement kept permanent residence by blacks in urban areas low, while facilitating the migratory labour system. The evolution of the rural populations in the various tribal areas has, therefore, had several features in common. Women in the various tribal areas participated in education and also formed part of the labour migratory flows. Their reproductive lives were strongly affected by these factors (Bozzoli and Nkotsoe 1991; Mayer and Mayer 1974). Apartheid settlement also reinforced settlement in accordance with the various ethnic groupings of the black population. The geographic areas allocated for settlement by the black population were, however, proportionately small, and this in due course became densely settled, with inadequate land and poverty.

The 1953 Tomlinson Report (Houghton 1956) provided a detailed account of the progressive deterioration of the rural subsistence economy of South Africa. The poverty also heightened the dependence of the rural populations on the growing modern sector of the economy. Both education and rapid social change coupled with rural-urban migration and family disruption are believed to have resulted in the erosion of the family system and the traditional reproductive norms.

It is difficult to judge the extent of the impact of the interventions of missionaries and colonial governments on the practices governing marriage and reproductive behaviour among the black population of South Africa. While bride-wealth continued to be given to legitimize marital unions, the decline in polygamous unions may have resulted both from religious conversions as well as from economic decline. The decline of polygamy that came about raised proportions of single women. Thus Mayer (1980) noted that Christian values, in discouraging polygamy, levirate, sororate and enforced marriage, raised the proportion of unmarried women in a context in which the merits of remaining celibate which Christianity expounded carried no conviction. The surplus of unmarried women led to widespread concubine unions in urban areas.

The impact of the introduction in South Africa of the National Family Planning Programme in 1975, with its Education, Information and Communication section, along with an extensive service network to both urban and rural women, was determined from the findings of 1987–89 Demographic and Health Survey. For the black rural population, increasing rural poverty and the weakened traditional accommodative capacity of families to shoulder the responsibility for large families may have contributed to women's positive response to childbirth regulation. Female-headed households had also become reality whose plight challenged both society and the state. The growth in women's education and their participation in the labour market, along with the expanding education and the concomitant cost of raising children may also have changed women's family size aspirations. Changes in reproductive behaviour are an important aspect of social change, signifying as they do a shift in the perceptions of the role of women in society, as well as a broadening of their self-perception beyond the reproductive role.

1.4 Definitions and Detailed Exposition of the Research Variables

The variables used in this research have been used in other analyses of reproductive behaviour dynamics. They however warrant some elaboration to establish their relevance and significance for this particular research. The discussion which follows provides such elaboration.

1.4.1 The Age Pattern of Onset of Childbearing

Age of a woman at onset of childbearing is a source of concern from a health, social developmental and demographic perspectives. Both early and late childbearing years have health risks for both the mother and the infant. In modern societies, early childbearing is also associated with interruption or termination of schooling, and thus with diminished opportunities for the woman's social development. From a demographic perspective, early onset of childbearing is associated with high completed parity, because of the available opportunities for subsequent births.

While acknowledging the high incidence of adolescent pre-marital childbirths in modern societies, demographic analyses continue to focus on marital age as indicative of the onset of reproductive behaviour. Such convergence between marriage and onset of childbearing appears to vary enormously across societies. The International Federation of Women Lawyers (1997) indicates considerable convergence between marriage and exposure of women to conception in Nigeria, where the median age at first marriage is 16 years and the average age of all women at first sexual intercourse is 15.9 years. The Federation notes that research done in Ethiopia in 1990 indicated that a third of women between ages 15–49 were married before the age of 15, while 41.1 per cent were married between ages of 15 and 17 years. Because of early onset of menarche among modern adolescents, early marriage is associated with early childbearing onset.

In South Africa, Wilson *et al.* (1952) reported that the age of women at marriage advanced from 19.3 years before 1890 to 23.6 years in the 1940s in the Keiskammahoek rural district of the Eastern Cape Province. It is, however, not clear whether this increase in marital age ever converged with an increase in age at onset of childbearing. Various estimates indicate that the age at onset of childbearing may have declined in recent years in South Africa.

Along with early childbearing are the problems of late childbearing and high parity. The Population Policy for South Africa (Department of Welfare 1998) describes South Africa's fertility structure as characterized by high-risk childbearing, explaining that women over 35 years of age and at parity of five and more accounted for 16 per cent of childbearing in 1993.

In this research, age at onset of childbearing is important from the social developmental, health and demographic perspectives, and the direction of its shift and its underlying determinants are therefore of analytic interest.

1.4.2 The Ages of Progression from First to Second and to Subsequent Births

The spacing of children is an important and resilient African tradition that emanates from an abhorrence of closely spaced childbirths. With regard to the spacing of childbirths, one might hypothesize drastic changes in the childbearing of the South African black women, even among rural women because of a noticeable pattern of long delays in progression to second childbearing after the first birth. This delay can be assumed to be facilitated by accessible contraception and motivated by career goals interrupted by the first pregnancy. In addition, this research hypothesizes that single women in particular delay progression to the second birth, and this phenomenon would be more pronounced among younger age cohorts. The delayed progression to the second birth is probably associated with pre-marital childbearing and a need by the affected women to postpone a second birth until they have entered into a marital union. Wide spacing of childbirths has endogenous origins in the population considered, and its survival would be indicative of some accommodative features of the changes in traditional reproductive norms.

1.4.3 The Number of Children Ever Born to Women

The number of children born per woman may indicate the pattern and pace of change in the reproductive behaviour of women. Such change also has social developmental implications for both the women and the children born. Childbearing demands considerable effort and time from women, and to a considerable extent rules out wider social participation and developmental activities. Too many childbirths may also impose challenges on household as well as on national resources. The number of childbirths per woman is also one of the focal aspects both from women's health and from a demographic perspective. As noted earlier, the latter aspect, however, generates conflict between the advocates for reproductive rights and those for population control in this discussion.

1.4.4 Marriage and Childbearing

Marriage is the traditional context within which demographers analyze women's reproductive behaviour. Burch (1983) explains that marriage legitimizes cohabitation and regular sexual intercourse between two or more adults, to provide socially approved reproduction, where the offspring enjoy full rights and privileges in relation to their parents, the kinship group and the larger society. LeVine and Scrimshaw (1983), however, point out that anthropologists have mating patterns as one of their classical areas of interest, a fact which draws them beyond examining marital fertility to non-marital fertility and dissolution of unions in their study of the reproductive behavioural patterns of societies.

Smith (1983) outlines various perspectives on the relationship between marriage and childbirth in both developed and developing societies. He describes marriage patterns as constituted by both timing and prevalence, that is, age at marriage and proportions ever marrying. Marital structure, on the other hand, describes the proportions never or ever married by age. Smith argues that rising mean ages at marriage and rising percentages of single persons reduce birth rates over any given period. Still, he notes that definitions of marriage are not consistent across societies. For Smith, later marriage is observed to influence childbirths through reduction of the duration of the woman's fecund exposure to sexual activity, attrition of the cohort that will survive to marry, reduction of tempo of population change through extension of mean length of a generation, and a change in period fertility. Smith's discussion thus assumes celibacy among unmarried women and makes no reference to fertility arising from informal reproductive unions that occur in some societies.

In contrast to Smith's exposition, Burch (1983) distinguishes between consensual and legal unions, noting studies that indicate a varying predominance and duration of each type of union in different societies and according to age groups. He notes that research on the fertility impact of consensual unions yielded contradictory findings, because of the instability of such unions, which is believed to reduce women's exposure to conception, thus reducing childbirths. In South Africa, Karim, Karim and Nkomokazi (1991 cited in Caldwell and Caldwell 1993) found that married women in a township peripheral to Durban averaged 4.1 childbirths, compared to 2.6 among unmarried women. This difference between marital and non-marital fertility could be of critical significance in the analyses of reproductive dynamics in South Africa. Statistics South Africa's 1995 October Household Survey revealed that nationally, 29 per cent of all women who had given birth at some time in their lives had never been married. This percentage among rural women was 33 per cent. The lower rate of childbearing among the substantial proportion of women who reproduce outside stable unions invariably contributes towards a lower overall fertility.

The argument that women in polygamous unions tend to have fewer children compared to those in monogamous unions has yet to be investigated. This is apparently attributable to their lower exposure to conception. Writing in 1931 about marriages among Xhosa women in the Eastern Cape, Soga expressed reservations about the alleged lower fertility among women in polygamous unions, although his position was based only on observation.

The assumed link between marriage and onset of childbearing among rural women in South Africa is challenged by the findings of the 1995 October Household Survey, which indicated a tenuous link between marriage and childbearing. However, among black women, the incidence of first child-births which occur to single women only provides a vague indication of the incidence of single motherhood, because formalization of marriages frequently follows a time schedule that is independent of childbearing.

South Africa is however known to have a long history of high pre-marital fertility, particularly among the black and coloured populations, as indicated in the Population Policy for South Africa (Department of Welfare1998). Anthropologists cited this situation as far back as the 1930s. Krige (1936) estimated the percentage of premarital births among blacks at a Pretoria township at 40 per cent in 1933–4 and at 59 per cent between 1934–5. Bozzoli and Nkontsoe's (1991) study among rural Tswana women in Phokeng also revealed that for the majority of women, childbearing began before and continued through marriage. Despite the persistence of pre-marital childbearing, research interest on its dynamics has waned, and recent debate has focused on the age of women at onset of childbearing.

In this research, the link between marriage and childbearing serves the purpose of highlighting the incidence of non-marital childbearing and bringing it into the analytic arena alongside marital childbearing.

1.4.5 Fertility Regulation

Fertility regulation by various means is integral to the consideration of women's reproductive behaviour. It is determined by the demand for children, which in turn is mediated by a variety of factors, such as knowledge of and accessibility of methods of regulating childbirths, attitudes, cultural values and psychic costs, as well as decision-making capacity. Even though sexual abstinence, particularly post-partum abstinence, is an important reproductive aspect of women's reproductive behaviour, it is excluded from this research which focuses on recorded information. Within the virulent AIDS epidemic context prevailing in South Africa, voluntary sexual abstinence probably plays a growing role in reproductive patterns, but its extent is difficult to determine. The 1998 SADHS by Department of Health, Medical Research Council, and Macri International reflected large proportions of women of reproductive age who responded that they do not use contraception because they are not sexually active. But conversely, the high incidence of rape in South Africa causes many women who are not sexually active to use contraception to protect themselves from conception in the event of being raped.

In the context of this research, contraception excludes traditional methods and encompasses the methods provided by family planning clinics and other service points. The use of service records also prescribes the exclusion of condoms, since they are not recorded on the service records of contraception clients. The methods considered are mostly hormonal but include intra-uterine devices (IUDs). Pregnancy terminations and sterilization which also contribute to the fertility regulation scenario are considered as separate variables from contraception in this research. Given below is a detailed discussion of these methods.

1.4.5.1 Contraception

Contraception is playing a very significant role in the reproductive changes amongst developing societies. Oosthuizen (1997) emphasized the fact that contraception played a relatively minor role in the European fertility decline that began a century before modern contraceptives became available. Conversely, the role of contraception has been more pronounced in the subsequent fertility transitions in Asia, Latin America and lately African countries.

Modern contraception makes up postponement of childbearing, reasonably deliberate child-spacing and parity-specific limiting of births practical realities. Research in developing societies has, however, revealed a number of socio-cultural, psychological, cognitive, cost, administrative, and health barriers to contraception. As with other forms of innovation, the diffusion of contraception into different cultures initially confronts what appear to be insurmountable barriers, but over time, the barriers slowly yield the way to diffusion. As individual societies overcome such barriers, they benefit more from the use of contraception.

The use of contraception in developing societies has been greatly facilitated by what Retherford and Palmore (1983) have described as purposive diffusion. Such diffusion involves the establishment of diffusion agencies, which are strategically located family planning clinics, and formulation and implementation of strategies to induce adoption in the service area. Diffusion strategies include infrastructure provision, affordable pricing, and optimal market selection and segmentation.

Access to contraception has over the years changed from receiving the advocacy of elite women and an insignificant proportion of male sympathizers to where it is subsumed as a human right. Women's reproductive health and reproductive rights were integral to the debates at the 1994 International Conference on Population and Development that was held in Cairo. The Programme of Action which came from the conference deliberations committed governments to the promotion of women's reproductive rights and reproductive health, in which information and access to contraception are integral (Population Council 1995).

In South Africa, the 1995 October Household Survey (Statistics South Africa 1995) found that 61 per cent of black reproductive age women nationally were currently using a method of modern contraception at the time of the survey. The 1998 South African Demographic and Health Survey (Department of Health, Medical Research Council, and Macri International 1998), gave a figure of 58.6 per cent, with 52.4 per cent for non-urban black women and 63.6 per cent for their urban counterparts, indicating a margin of almost 11 per cent between the two groups, which might be suggestive of differential access to reproductive health services.

1.4.5.2 HIV/AIDS, Condom Use and Sexual Abstinence

AIDS prevention entails the use of condoms, which are incidentally a barrier method of contraception. Sexual abstinence prompted by AIDS awareness also contributes to reduced conceptions. The South African Demographic and Health Survey (*ibid.*) also found a significant percentage of South African women in their reproductive years (22.5 per cent) who reported having had no sexual partner in the preceding twelve months. Such sexual abstinence might be related to AIDS awareness. Reported sexual abstinence as a reason for not using contraception was contained in the data of the two surveys used in this research, as well as condom use. This information is not, however, available on the data collected from the 2004 service records.

1.4.5.3 Voluntary Sterilization

Sterilization contributes significantly to childbirth regulation in some national family planning programmes. Its virtue lies in that it reduces the risks associated with late childbearing and high parity, since women use it when the required number of children has been achieved.

The 1998 South African Demographic and Health Survey findings revealed that nearly 70 per cent of women interviewed knew about female sterilization as a method of contraception and 12 per cent had used it. The United Nations Fund for Population Activities (1997) however commented that in South Africa, sterilization services are often logistically difficult for women to access, and that there is a large unmet need for female sterilization. The contribution of this variable to the reproductive changes occurring in the subject population is also of analytic interest.

1.4.5.4 Pregnancy Terminations

Pregnancy terminations as a method of regulating childbirths have a long history. David (1983) cites evidence that suggests that nearly everywhere, women of all backgrounds resort to abortion to some extent, regardless of legal codes, religious sanctions or personal dangers. Among the earliest concessions to abortion, he cites Aristotle's recommendation of abortion as a means of maintaining the ideal population size of a city-state wherever couples already had sufficient children. Despite its long history and universality across cultures, controversy about its moral legitimacy continues unabated, and David notes, "No other elective surgical procedure has generated as much worldwide debate, generated such emotional and moral controversy, or received greater sustained attention from members of the public concerned with women's rights and well being"(David 1983, 193).

The illegality of abortion in some societies as well as the social ambivalence and political sensitivity that attaches to it have inhibited research on its contribution to the regulation of childbirths. In South Africa, the Abortion Repeal Action Group, a non-governmental organization, dedicated efforts to monitoring and making public the incidence of illegal abortions as part of lobbying the government to liberalize abortion. The promulgation of the Termination of Pregnancy Act, (Republic of South Africa: Choice on Termination of Pregnancy Act No 92 of 1996) came on 12 November 1996. The "Choice Act," as it is frequently referred to, has put South Africa ahead of sub-Saharan African countries in progressive abortion legislation. This legislation, along with other legislation on the rights of women, could be viewed as indicative of the commitment of the new government to removing obstacles to women's reproductive rights, as well as to the social and economic advancement of women. Legislation liberalizing abortion occurred in the face of substantial opposition from pro-life and other interest groups in South Africa. The Choice Act defines the circumstances in which a pregnancy may lawfully be terminated, as well as the penalties for contravening the requirements of this law. It also regulates abortion information.

In the face of these developments, pregnancy termination has now emerged as a subject for analysis in women's regulation of their reproductive behaviour in South Africa, and such analyses are emerging. The findings of a study conducted by the Reproductive Research Unit (1997) in Soweto indicated that termination of pregnancy (TOP) services are used predominantly by younger clients at high school and post-matric. The present research incorporates as a variable the requests for TOP services across age cohorts in the population of women under consideration.

1.4.5.5 Decision Making on Childbearing

International legislative influence on human rights has tried over the years to protect couple and women's decision-making control on childbearing. As far back as the 1968 Teheran Conference on Human Rights, the international community agreed, "Parents have a basic human right to decide freely and responsibly on the number and spacing of their children and a right to adequate education and information in this respect" (United Nations 1968).

In further support of its position, in 1979, the United Nations, in Article 16 of the Convention on the Elimination of All Forms of Discrimination Against Women (CEDAW), explicitly codified women's right to reproductive decision-making as follows: "States parties shall take all appropriate measures to ... ensure on a basis of equality of men and women ... the same right to decide freely and responsibly on the number and spacing of their children and to have access to the information, education and means to enable them to exercise these rights" (United Nations 1979).

These international agreements have been ratified by many developing countries, including South Africa. Even though they are in conflict with social traditions, they are viewed favourably by women as facilitative of their reproductive choices. But the agreements are also significant elements in the debate on exogenous and endogenous origins of change, and whether reproductive changes in developing countries can be viewed as evolutionary.

The role of traditional power relations as a determinant of reproductive behaviour may be declining in contemporary societies. This is demonstrated by the Choice Act in South Africa, which does not require parental consent for a minor wishing to have a pregnancy termination. Thus, while South African parents may influence the reproductive decisions of their minor children, their opinions have no legal force.

The extent to which men dominate reproductive decision-making is, however, unknown. The payment of *lobola* (bride-wealth) in accordance to African custom gives the bridegroom and his family rights over the reproductive capacity of the woman. In writing about Xhosa customs and traditions, Soga (1931) is equivocal in linking lobola to women's childbearing capacity and emphasizes the protection lobola gives the woman against abuse. The perceived entitlement of husbands to progeny on payment of lobola is reflected in the responses of males interviewed by Van der Vliet in her 1982 study of black marriages. One respondent discredits companionship as a rationale for his marriage as follows: "I married my wife so that she can give birth to my children .... For my happiness I have to go outside and look for another woman" (cited in Van der Vliet 1982, 183). In the same research, another male interviewee has said this the role of lobola, "... a man must pay lobola and have children to increase his family" (*ibid. 55*).

The extent to which African men in South Africa assert their right to progeny on the basis of their payment of lobola has never been investigated. What has been noted, however, is that some women conceal their using family planning from their reproductive partners (Preston-Whyte 1988), hence the preference among black women for injection as a method of contraception. The 1998 South African Demographic and Health Survey findings observed that injection is by far the most commonly used method, being used by 57 per cent of all women. However, confidentiality may not be the only reason for the popularity of this method.

The Bill of Rights promulgated in the 1994 Constitution of South Africa further protects the individual's right to decide on sexual and reproductive behaviour in Section 2 (9) 2 as follows:

> Everyone has the right to psychological and bodily integrity, which includes the right-
>
> > (a) to make decisions concerning reproduction; and
> >
> > (b) to security and control over their body.

The Bill of Rights thus ignores the traditional childbearing expectations inherent in bridal wealth payments. However, commenting on human rights and reproductive choice in general, Freedman and Isaacs (1993) note that changes in laws are a necessary but not sufficient condition for improvement in the quality of people's rights. It can thus be argued that the question of reproductive decision-making among the black women of South Africa hangs precariously between the traditional world, which denies the woman decision-making powers and the progressive world of human rights legislation that confers to the woman decision-making powers over her reproductive behaviour. Women face the challenge of navigating their way through these two worlds.

In this research, this variable was included to determine changes in women's participation in decision-making on childbearing. This would indicate a movement away from the traditional situation of women in this regard, but, as indicated earlier, would be consistent with both the national constitutional dispensation and international agreements on human rights.

1.5 Summary of the Critical Elements of this Research

The discussion in this introductory chapter gave an exposition of changes in women's reproductive behaviour in various societies as a subject of analytic interest and the evolution of the various theoretical rationales for fertility regulation. The objectives of the present research were outlined as analytic and descriptive, and the intended focal aspects for analytic attention were identified. The various socio-historical, demographic and other features of the subject population were then explored, and the research variables located within that context.

CHAPTER 2
LITERATURE REVIEW

The first section of this review departs from a universalistic outlook on regulation of childbearing and explores literature sources that provide expositions of the background of childbirth regulation as a societal practice, along with the initial social resistances to its strengthening by modern technology. Expositions of the unfolding dominance at different periods of the human rights, health and demographic rationales for regulation of childbearing were explored. The dominance of the demographic rationale during the recent decades, until the watershed at the 1994 Cairo Conference on Population and Development received attention. Also literature sources on the new paradigm which makes women's empowerment central to reproductive behavioural discourses and requires governmental accountability for the prescribed interventions were explored.

The second section of the review focused on the unfolding of the socio-cultural dimensions that have played a significant role in shaping women's reproductive behaviour in African societies. This section departs from a cultural relativist perspective, focusing on analyses of the works that highlight the prescriptive voice of African norms and traditions, and their interplay with the forces of change in the reproductive behaviour of African women in general, and that of the women in the research population in particular. Literature discourses that acknowledge the African cultural commonalities across African societies in women's reproductive patterns and their background cosmology were outlined. This section also gives much more prominence to women's discourses on women's reproductive behaviour changes, although male's perspectives were also cited. Discourses that centre on the value accorded to children, the cultural reactions to childlessness, the number and sex of children born, the emotional, material, and social benefits of childbearing, the notion of fertility regulation, marriage as the locus of women's reproduction, and the societal reactions to childbearing that occur outside marriage were explored. Added to that, the review of the second section makes specific focus on recent analyses of the reproductive changes amongst the black population of South Africa.

2.1 Some Expositions on the Regulation of Childbearing as a Societal Practice

Thomas (1989) cites various historical approaches used by ancient societies to regulate rates of childbirth. While the ancient Romans adopted reproductive practices directed at increasing their population, encouraging early marriage and discouraging celibacy, Contrary to that, ancient Greeks and Spartan society leaders before them were anxious about overpopulation and implemented what Thomas describes as "stony-hearted policies." Thomas also points out that Lamaist Buddhists contributed a son from each family to Buddhist monasteries, thereby reducing the number of reproductive males in their societies, while the practice of polyandry in Tibet also reduced childbirths. Thomas adds that many families in the agricultural past limited the number of births through *coitus interruptus*, postponement of marriage, sexual abstinence, abortion and infanticide, and that limiting children helped families in agricultural societies to avoid division of properties. He thus rightly concludes that it is foolish to suppose that the idea of contraception is a modern one.

Gordon (1977), on the other hand, argues that birth control was not invented by scientists or doctors but by women as part of the folklore and folk culture of nearly all societies. This is the universalistic notion of childbirth regulation. Traditional practices on women's regulation of childbearing have been one of the subjects of interest for anthropologists and historians. The diverse patterns of women's reproductive behaviour exhibited by contemporary societies are part of a long history of regulatory mechanisms of individuals, couples and societies to influence the reproduction of human life in one direction or the other. Also Hartmann (1995) argues that the human race has long sought to control births, using abstinence, withdrawal, abortion and infanticide, along with barrier methods like condoms, cervical caps and vaginal sponges.

However, writing during the early 20th century on the reproductive traditions of the Xhosa population of South Africa, Soga observed as follows, "The question of birth control which has been exercising the minds of its advocates in the most civilized countries in Europe finds no echo among the Bantu, and especially among Bantu women. With them procreation is not only a divine institution, but also a natural obligation" (Soga 1931, 289).

Burman's exposition on the practice of abortion at the micro-level (1990, 48–51), however, points to evidence that African women may have concealed their fertility regulatory activities from public view, in desperate efforts to conform to the norms of their societies. In addition, external sex was a widely known and accepted practice for avoiding the occurrence of unintended pregnancies amongst Africans. Notenstein's (1953) postulation that peasant societies throughout the world were organized in ways that brought pressure on their members to reproduce themselves to offset high mortality is inadequately substantiated. Rather it appears that traditional societies had a variety of views on optimal reproductive behaviour, and that within those contexts, women frequently played out their personal and private reproductive agendas.

2.1.1 The Unfolding of Scientific Childbearing Regulation

This research hinged on the expanding role accorded to the scientific methods of childbirth regulation or family planning in the research population considered. Gordon (1977) notes that during the second decade of the 20th century, a new philosophy of sex radicalism led to sexuality being valued independently of reproduction, and voluntary motherhood was viewed as a desirable goal for childbearing regulation. Hartmann (1995) points out that despite various limitations, the associations and organizations that supported the introduction of contraception played a valuable role in making it more accessible and available, thus freeing many women from the burden of unwanted pregnancies. During the course of its evolution, the Planned Parenthood Federation emphasized its concern with population growth and later became linked to the American Eugenics Society, an institution that incorporated family planning and abortion in a racist agenda that ultimately found a resounding expression in Nazi Germany. Hartmann (*ibid*) argues that eugenicists and racists turned birth control into an offensive tool of top-down planning in what she describes as the post-War population control, which was based on the demographic rationale for childbearing regulation. In the post-War era, the most ardent proponents of childbearing regulation came from a neo-Malthusian perspective, which perceived a strong link between population and poverty, a subject that has engaged an enduring intellectual debate.

For Hartmann, from the 1950s onwards, large amounts of money flowed into what some observers have described as "a powerful cult of population control." Links with Third World leadership and officials, medical personnel and academics both in the United States and elsewhere were established. Soon, the United Nations, through its United Nations Fund for Population Activities (UNFPA 1997), the World Bank, the United States Agency for International Development (USAID) and various private agencies were all lined up into a formidable edifice that was replete with an arsenal of strategies for stabilizing the populations of developing countries. At the 1984 World Population Conference that was held in Bucharest, specific targets for world population stabilization were set. There was, however, opposition from some developing countries to the view that population growth, rather than underdevelopment, was the problem, as well as calls for a new economic order (Hartmann 1995).

Although the three rationales for childbearing regulation appear to be mutually supportive, it has been demonstrated in evaluations of programmes based on the demographic rationale that the health and human rights of women are often undermined in the implementation of strategies based on the demographic rationale. Such violations have been the source of scathing criticisms of the demographic rationale. In her analysis of the evolution of the Indonesian demographic "success story", Hartmann (*ibid*) pointed to weaknesses like limitations of contraceptive choice, coercion of women into using supposedly more effective methods, inadequate infrastructure for treatment of side effects and for routine checks of women with intra-uterine devices (IUDs) and for long-term checks for monitoring of hormonal contraceptive users, as well as penalties for using traditional rather than modern methods. Hartmann also criticizes the use of authority, in which central commands produced compliant behaviour "all down the administrative line to the individual peasant." In some areas of Indonesia, the military and the police reportedly became directly involved in promoting IUD insertion, and family planning acceptors felt pressurized to accept contraceptive measures which they did not want to use, in a rush to achieve childbirth reduction targets. In addition, Hartmann notes the flawed use of incentives for compliance to regulation of births, arguing that amongst desperately poor people with limited choices, being offered food or money as a reward for sterilization cannot realistically and justly be considered as being offered a choice. She also notes that demographers have been cautious about attributing Indonesia's fertility decline to family planning, but have instead pointed to a number of broad social and economic changes that included a rise in male and female educational achievement, declining infant mortality, urbanization and changing patterns of rural employment that are conducive to smaller families. She also argues that in the case of Kenya, the emergence of fertility decline is attributed to pressure on land, educational and social mobility, and the emergence of more economic independence for women.

Despite the criticism levelled at the demographic approach to regulation of childbirths, its effect in reducing the pace of population growth and in changing reproductive patterns is roundly acknowledged. During the apartheid years, South Africa remained outside the reach of the international sphere of population and reproductive regulation activity discussed previously. However, the questions about the growth of the black and largest component of the South African population generated considerable anxiety for the apartheid government. The Science Committee on Population and Development that was convened in 1984 also raised concerns about poverty and environmental resources. The Population Development Programme that was set up in 1985 was driven by the same demographic agenda as the international population establishment. It was also separated from the National Family Planning Programme, which was set up ten years earlier, and was based on the health rationale. Many of the criticisms applied to the population control programmes set up elsewhere were similarly levelled at the Population Development Programme in South Africa.

2.1.2 The 1994 New Population and Development Paradigm

South Africa's political change to democracy coincided with the 1994 Cairo Conference on Population and Development, in which a new and less controversial path for addressing population growth and poverty was inaugurated by the international community, amid extensive deliberations and horse trading. The Programme of Action that governments and non-governmental organizations arrived at during the 1994 Cairo Conference reflected an ideological shift from a population control outlook with a narrow focus on the regulation of women's reproduction that was subject to persistent criticisms for its disregard of women's rights and wilful pursuit of targets. The new approach to regulation of childbirths broadly encompasses considerations of sexual and reproductive health and the reproductive rights of women, including adolescents (Johnson 1995). The Programme of Action aims at mobilizing governments to view women's reproductive behaviour within the broader context of women's improved status, along with women's educational, economic, and other realities that impact on their capacity to make sexual and reproductive decisions. The new approach considers women's overall empowerment as the core within which the demographic, human rights and health rationales for childbearing regulation should find their expression in the provision of reproductive health services.

2.2 Tradition and Change in African Women's Childbearing Behaviour

Ngubane (1977) points out that a good knowledge of what people change from is a prerequisite for understanding the directions of transformation. This section of the review draws heavily from African literary works and from anthropological analyses of tradition and change in African women's childbearing. These sources complement each other's evaluations of the various aspects of women's reproduction that this research focuses on. Emecheta's work (1979) enjoys the privileged position of providing an African woman's perspective on most of the variables considered in this research, while Soga (1931), Mphahlele (1979), Head (1984), and others also add their perspectives on specific aspects. As far as possible, this section of the review also provides descriptions of the baseline scenario of rural black women's reproductive patterns among the subject populations, along with the interactions between traditions and social change, and the impact of such interactions on women's reproductive behaviour scenario analyzed in this research. Literature that evaluates the traditions for their implications for the societies in general, and for women in particular was also explored.

On African women's reproductive traditions, Nhlapo (1991) points out that the overriding values of the traditional African family are reflected in the non-individual nature of marriage, the goals of procreation subsumed in marriage, which are economic survival and security. He observes that the need to procreate prescribes attitudes to barrenness, sororate, levirate, child betrothal, and forced marriage. He notes further that in patriarchal societies, group interests are framed in favour of men and that in marriage, men acquire rights over women and children through payment of bride-price. It is within that context that women are adjuncts to the group, a means by which the overriding goals of clan survival are achieved.

Nhlapo's exposition echoes the observations made by Guy (1990, 40), that the control and appropriation of the productive and reproductive capacity of women was central to the structure of southern Africa's pre-capitalistic societies. However, as suggested by Nhlapho, this feature is not confined to the southern African region, but is contained in the broader African cultural context as well. Thus, Mishra (1983) noted that in Kenya, socially and culturally, women were made to see their primary role in life as the production of children, and that it is through marriage, pregnancy and motherhood that they could find dignity and respect. This can be linked to Hartmann's general observation that men have very little economic incentive to want fewer children, since women bear most of the responsibility for child support (Hartmann 1995).

Caldwell and Caldwell (1987) associate the pro-natalist traditional African reproductive values with the traditional belief in ancestors, which attributes extreme importance to succession of generations and considers the risk of family extinction to be unacceptable. The Caldwells (*ibid*) argue that in African traditions, religious underpinnings are the major determinant of reproduction over and above economic considerations, and that barrenness is a matter of social and theological significance. In practice, this means that poor economic circumstances of parents cannot discourage reproduction in African societies in the way they do in other societies, because children are viewed as wealth in and of themselves. Accordingly, the Caldwells note that the fear of a wife who seeks to control her own reproduction is not of breaking a socially recognized contract, but of angering her husband's ancestors, thereby causing suffering to herself and her children.

Emecheta (1979) epitomized the African woman's reproductive scenario outlined earlier in the life of Nnu Ego, who internalized the marital and reproductive demands prescribed by the traditions of her society, lived by them through difficult times until she died in abject poverty and desperation. In the reproductive milestones that spanned Nnu Ego's life, her father found a marriage suitor for her, received the mandatory bride-price and married her away with all the pomp that befits the daughter of a respectable man. The marriage was, however, ruined when she could not beget children, and she was humiliated when her husband married a second wife who promptly delivered the required male offspring. Subjected to mistreatment by her husband, Nnu Ego finally returned to her family, and her father returned the bride-wealth he had received on her account.

Nnu Ego's father found another suitor for her, and this time the bride wealth was amply rewarded with what, even to Nnu Ego, seemed to be an uncontrollable flow of childbirths. She faced the agony of infant deaths twice, and nearly committed suicide when her first child died–it was a male child. The second loss involved a female child, and Nnu Ego felt guilty that the loss of the child did not touch her as deeply as the first one did. Nnu Ego never regulated her childbirths by any means, and believed her *chi* (which seems to be the counterpart of a guardian angel) to be in control of her childbearing destiny. Her life was spent in abject poverty and endless efforts to provide for her children. Despite the difficult circumstances, she managed to pay for the education of her two sons, and the bride–wealth received from her daughters' marriages was absorbed into the successful education of her sons, while the daughters were set on the path of marriage and childbearing that African tradition prescribed for them.

Emecheta's Nnu Ego provides the background for the review of literature sources on the traditions of childbearing amongst African women. The review explores perspectives on the salient aspects of women's childbearing in African traditions and how the debates on childbearing regulation discussed in the first section of this review have impinged on them. Marriage and its various ramifications provide the core of this section of the review. Also literature sources on non-marital childbearing, which is a growing factor in the subject population of rural women are explored.

2.2.1 *Marriage as the Traditional Locus of Childbearing in African Societies*

As in other societies, marriage is the traditional locus of women's childbearing in African societies. It is formalized through the transfer of bride-wealth by the groom and his family to the family of the bride. This tradition has reflected tremendous resilience in Southern Africa, and documentation of its traditional dynamics across African societies is explored in the following sub-section.

2.2.1.1 *Bride-wealth and its Attendant Reproductive Obligations for African Women*

Bride-wealth underpins African women's marriage and reproduction, as African writers indicate in their story lines. Somalia's Nuruddin (1970) creates a girl who is betrayed by her grandfather and guardian, who accepted camels as bride-wealth from an old man on her account. Egypt's Nawal Saadawi similarly includes bride-wealth negotiations in her Woman at Point Zero narrative (1983). Writing about Xhosa traditions in South Africa, Soga (1931) explains that her father regards a girl or young woman as the family's wealth in cattle. In addition to constituting wealth to the father or guardian, bride-wealth imposes child-bearing obligations that have no defined limit on the woman upon marriage, a fact which underlies its relevance to this discussion. Radcliffe-Brown and Forde (1965) explain that an African marries because he wants children, and that the most important part of the 'value' of a woman is her child-bearing capacity. As a result her kin will either return the marriage payment or provide her husband with another woman to bear children, if a married woman turns out to be barren. Vaughn (1994) echoes this observation, adding that so closely is bride-wealth tied to children that typically, in the event of marital dissolution, it must be returned in proportion to the number of children born in the marriage. Hence, Emecheta (1979) is specific about the fact that Nnu Ego's father paid back to her former husband the bride-wealth he had received for her daughter, before proceeding to finding another suitor for her and accepting bride-wealth from him.

Armstrong *et al* (1993) explain that bride-wealth grants the husband rights over the woman's procreative capacity. Clark and Van Heerden (1992) note that in South Africa, customary law prescribes that a child born to a widow, irrespective of its paternity, belongs to the deceased husband's family. This, they explain, is the logical extension of the rule that the payment of bride-wealth transfers rights in respect of progeny from the wife to the husband's family. Guy (1990, 41) adds the observation that in African traditions, the progenitor of the child was often of little social significance, and that an absent, impotent or even dead man could still become a father. This aspect has, however, been challenged by both the church and some African leaders in Southern Africa. Head (1984) recounts how Chief Khama, in his various reforms of traditional ways among the BamaNgwato tribe of the Tswana group, made it a rallying point in reforming women's position in his society. In this analysis, bride wealth payment has relevance in so far as it provides a partial explanation of the differential childbearing patterns between married and single women.

2.2.1.2 Polygamy, Levirate in African Women's Childbearing Traditions

Marriage in the traditional African context includes polygamy, which Soga (1931) described as universal among the tribes of Bantu origin. Vaughn (1994) adds that in approximately 97 per cent of African societies, polygamy is traditionally preferred. According to Tabah (1989), the institution of polygamy had a specific purpose of keeping women in their reproductive years in unions, and therefore is consistent with the traditional pro-natal outlook of African societies. Tabah also emphasized that the purpose of African marriage is procreation, and that when dissolutions of unions occur, women enter into other unions and are not left alone as they often are in other cultures. Caldwell and Caldwell (1987) note that constraints on fertility in African societies have been overcome by early and universal female marriage, pressure on widows of reproductive age to remarry quickly, if possible by levirate or polygamy.

Women's reactions to polygamy have varied enormously, and educated women in particular have tended to have a jaundiced view of it. In Mphahlele's Chirundu, the prospective polygamist husband is puzzled at what it is about an educated woman that causes a resentment of polygamy (Mphahlele 1979). The woman writer Ba (1980) recounts how she grudgingly accepted the intrusion of a second wife, 30 years into her marriage, while her friend walked out of her marriage under similar circumstances. Both of Nnu Ego's marriages developed into polygamous unions, the first one because she could not reproduce promptly, and the second one because her second husband inherited two widows from a deceased brother. In his advanced years, Nnu Ego's husband married a sixteen year-old girl. Nnu Ego accepted the last co-wife in quiet submission to tradition, but not before confronting her husband in exasperation about the dire economic circumstances of their household with saying, "Have you gone mad or something? We have only one room to share with my five children and I am expecting another two; yet you brought another person" (Emecheta1979, 184).

The practice of levirate provided for one of the brothers to take over both the conjugal and economic responsibilities of the deceased in the household of the new widow. The acceptability of this arrangement to women also varied. Ba (*ibid*) would not succumb to the practice and states that her voice that had known 30 years of silence burst out in angry protest against the proposed intrusion in her life by her brother-in-law, urging him to purge himself of his dreams of conquest, because she would not become his wife. Levirate is almost unknown in the contemporary South African marital and reproductive patterns, even though the retention of customary law leaves the door open for the practice. Also Polygamy is rare. Their relevance to this research emanates from the fact that they traditionally shielded women from non-marital childbearing, which has become a common phenomenon in Southern Africa. Since women shoulder most of the economic responsibility of raising children in the traditional African family, the question of their role in decision-making on both marriage and reproduction arises, and this review turned to that aspect.

2.2.1.3 Power Relations in African Marital and Reproductive Decisions

Even though Soga (1931) implied that the parental prerogative of selecting a spouse applied only where Xhosa daughters were concerned. Other narratives on Xhosa society indicate that it applied to sons as well (Peteni 1976; Jordaan 1980; Mandela 1994). In all the narratives cited, however, the sons were successfully recalcitrant to such impositions, sometimes with tragic consequences. Women's recalcitrance to the imposition of spouses on the other hand was viewed as a threat to social order and encountered harsh reprisals (Fuze 1979; Guy 1990, 45). The 1993 Report of the Panel on Population Dynamics in sub-Saharan Africa indicates that although there is a reduction of parental control over marriage, leading to a growing autonomy in the choice of partner, especially among educated urban families, considerable proportions of uneducated and rural respondents reported that their husbands were chosen for them. Both of Nnu Ego's marriages were arranged by her father. Although she intensely disliked and despised the second spouse, she put up with him, fearful of putting her father to shame by undermining his authority (Emecheta 1979).

The payment of bride price in African culture also marks the transfer of legal power over the woman from her father to her husband and his lineage. The legal power referred to includes sexual and reproductive capacities as well as economic contributions. The extent to which these power relations are applied can be assumed to vary with different couples.

2.2.1.4 The Emotional and Economic Motivations for Child-bearing in African Traditions

The value of children in traditional African society cannot be sufficiently highlighted. Emecheta's Nnu Ego explained her desire for children to her father in the following statements, "When one grows old, one needs children to look after one. If you have no child and your parents have gone, who can you call your own?" (Emecheta 1979, 38).

This statement appears to suggest that children provide women with both material and emotional benefits. Childlessness conversely carries social stigma, particularly for women, and Nnu Ego expressed feelings of worthlessness in her appeals to the supernatural force she believed to be responsible for her plight in entreaties like, "Oh my chi, why do you bring me so low?"(Emecheta 1979, 32).

For men, children fulfill the desire and perceived male obligation to ensure the continuity of the clan. Thus, frustrated at Nnu Ego's incapacity to beget children, her first husband explained to her the reason for his urgent need for a second wife in clan survival terms. He had no time to waste his precious male seed on a woman who is infertile because he had to raise children for his line. If Nnu Ego could not produce sons, she had to help harvest yams.

The high demand for children in African traditions prompts the question of how the economic demands of raising children were met in traditional African societies In considering customary law in South Africa, Clark and van Heerden (1992) point out that children were regarded as economic assets, and the family to which they were affiliated simply absorbed them. Caldwell, Orobuloye, and Caldwell (1992) explained that the economics of the family and fertility applicable in western societies did not apply in the traditional African context for a number of reasons. Firstly, the authors pointed out, the traditional African outlook on childbearing did not assume children to be an economic liability to their father, and that in polygamous unions; the basic child-rearing economic unit was the mother and her dependent children. Secondly, they noted that biological bearing of children and the cost of child-raising were separated by a high incidence of child fostering. Thirdly, reproductive decision-making and the cost of child-rearing were separate. The father decided on child-bearing but was spared much of the cost of rearing children, even though he received material returns from his children throughout their lives until his death. Looking at the economic theories on child-bearing, Caldwell and Caldwell (1987) postulated the direction of wealth flows from children to parents as being at the heart of the resistance of African fertility patterns to change. They noted that African parents received larger and more certain rewards from reproduction than do parents in any other society, and that the upward wealth flows are guaranteed by interwoven social and religious sanctions. Caldwell, Orobuloye and Caldwell (1992) on their part noted that since widows had no claim to the deceased husbands' property, their security derived from their children. In view of this contingency, women desired a large surviving family, irrespective of its cost.

When hard times hit Emecheta's Nnu Ego and her large progeny, they progressively descended into abject poverty that made her extremely despondent, and despite her prolific reproduction, she asks herself, "What have I gained from all this? Yes, I have many children, but what do I have to feed them on? On my life. I have to work myself to the bone to look after them" (Emecheta 1979, 186).

Emecheta's narrative also points to the threat childbearing placed on the educational aspirations of Nnu Ego's eleven year old son, who, noticing her mother's size, realized that she was pregnant again. In his thoughts, the boy questioned why his parents kept adding new members to his family, despite the financial difficulties the family faced. Observing the abject poverty his family was living in, the boy feared that his aspirations to continue with school would come to nothing.

While reproduction in all societies normally occurs within marriage, the growing incidence of pre-marital and extra-marital reproduction in some societies makes it impossible to ignore this phenomenon in any discussion of women's reproductive behaviour which tries to be comprehensive.

2.2.2 African Traditions and the Emergence of Non-marital Childbearing

Among the Xhosa population of the Eastern Cape, Soga (1931) noted that traditionally, there were strong sanctions against both pre-marital and extra-marital childbearing. In this regard, Guy (1990, 42) adds that the control of the fertility of the unmarried in the research populations was intense and was given social prominence during the initiation ceremonies as well as in the ideology of deference imposed by the old on the young.

Hunter (1936) however raised contrary views on the traditional universality of marriage in the subject populations, and pointed out that women's life choices on marriage always diverged. She argued that for some women, marriage has always been experienced as an unsatisfactory life arrangement. Hunter's work among the Pondo ethnic group in the Transkei exposed her to a network of extra-marital relationships engaged in by both men and women. The relationships Hunter describes are similar to those seen in contemporary societies, which are often interpreted as signifying a moral degeneracy associated with westernization. More significantly for this research, Hunter describes the existence in traditional Pondo society of women called *amadikazi,* who either had children outside marriage, or had opted out of marriage, or were widowed and decided to return to their natal families. She describes these women as "always noticeable by the number of their ornaments and the elegance of their clothes presented by their lovers" (Hunter 1936, 206).

The women depicted wanted a much easier life than what marriage could offer in the traditional male-female relationships, and can be viewed as precursors of the non-marital childbearing scenario of the contemporary context in the subject populations. The South African marital scenario, in which growing proportions of women cautiously avoid marriage is depicted by van der Vliet, (1991), and has similarities to what is described in Botswana by Schapera (1971) and Gulbrandsen (1986). These scenarios were historically part of the marital scenario in the population considered in this research. Traditional wedding songs depicted marriage as a monumental challenge for women specifically, with marital traditions demanding the woman's singularly stoical discipline, whose rationale was often beyond the grasp of some women. Among the Tswana, Gulbrandsen explains that the category of women who remain unmarried mothers are denoted as wise women. It should thus not come as a surprise that with the collapse of gerontocratic pressure to marry, substantial proportions of women select not to marry.

Gulbrandsen, however, considers the ambivalence of both Tswana men and women to enter into marital unions as arising from life styles, and explains that "there has been a dramatic transformation in the idioms of rank, resulting in marriage not only becoming irrelevant, but even "just causing trouble" in the young men's achievements. Marriage means that a young man might be 'hampered' all the time by a wife who "makes a noise" when he comes home, and who may even bring a case against him because of poor maintenance (Gulbrandsen 1986, 15).

Gulbrandsen notes that the economic responsibilities young Tswana men have for supporting their natal families and the economic dependence of mothers and sisters on the young man's income generate resentment of the economic implications of his marriage and may create an unwelcome environment for his wife. Within that scenario, Timaeus and Graham (1989, 391) commented on the likely emergence in Botswana society of an elderly group of men who have never married and have no legitimate children.

The analysis of patterns of non-marital childbearing in African societies is at its primacy. This might be because the existence of polygamy and gerontocratic pressure on the formation of reproductive unions have held ground for longer in most African societies than elsewhere. The growing participation by women in education and their capacity to earn incomes, however, appears to offer them choices and makes them question marital unions, especially polygamous unions as an optimal social arrangement. Thus, Karanja (1994) documents the emergence of the phenomenon of "outside wives" among the Nigerian elite groups, constituted by women who opt for unions which have "no politico-jural status" because such unions are sanctioned by neither tradition nor statutory law. The unions Karanja describes are characterized by unidirectional wealth flows from 'husband' to partner, and have significantly lower birth rates than formal unions. It is unclear how widely spread the phenomenon of outside wives is. Still, it reflects the growing tendency of women to eschew traditional marriage as the locus of reproduction.

These analyses suggest that the growing incidence of non-marital childbearing in African societies is generating some analytic interest. The issues focused on have included its demographic implications, whether it affects certain socio-economic strata and age groups more than others, and whether it is a precursor to marriage or not in the societies affected.

2.2.3 Observations on Adolescent Childbearing

Where adolescent pre-marital childbearing is concerned, however, South African society may be out of step with other African societies in the lenient stance it adopts. In this regard, research by the Panel on Population Dynamics in Sub-Saharan Africa (1993) revealed that pregnancy among unmarried urban schoolgirls often ignited public outrage, with disapproval surfacing most visibly in policies that expel pregnant girls from school or screen them for admission to advanced education. The panel notes that powerful sanctions result in fears of condemnation which make adolescents shy away from reproductive health and child-care services. This situation contrasts sharply with what prevails in South Africa as vividly described by Preston-Whyte and Zondi thus: "To be unmarried and have a child does not blight one's future as it does or once did in a number of other milieus" (1992, 232).

Emecheta's (1979) Nnu Ego came from an "illegitimate" reproductive union between her unmarried mother and an *obi* or traditional leader who commanded a lot of respect, wealth, multiple wives and concubines. She was seen and accepted by everyone as the love-child of this respected man, because of a specific negotiated understanding entered into between the families of the two parties. Nnu Ego's biological father received bride wealth from the approved suitor and married her away with the pomp. The role played by her illegitimate father in her life is not unusual in the African cultural context, but also pertained to the specific circumstances which surrounded her deceased mother's life. The relationship between father and daughter remained strong until the father's death. Those who new her well in Lagos city called her "Daughter of Agbadi" and Nnu Ego would not do anything that would disgrace the name of her father.

2.3 Expositions of Changing Childbearing Patterns Amongst South African Blacks

From the traditional African reproductive scenario that has been outlined in the previous section, it is worthwhile to examine the discourses and analyses that place the specific directional changes followed by women's reproductive behaviour of the subject population into perspective. Many of these aspects are contained in the unfolding of the colonial history of the subject population and the cultural conflicts and ambivalences that attended diffusion of Christian values, education and economic changes.

Observing how the social organization of the black populations in South Africa had changed since they came into contact with the Westerners, Pauw (1976) noted a general weakening of the patrilineal kinship system, and the new social distinction which emerged between the conservative element of the black society and those who accepted the churches, schools and other aspects of western culture. While this literature review now focused on the latter group or "school people" that spearheaded the changes in women's reproductive patterns, also the "red people" were discussed as a reference group that demonstrates the course women's reproductive behaviour might have followed without the exogenous influences indicated. The Xhosa ethnic population of the Eastern Cape was used as an example of this phenomenon and the women's reproductive changes that were embedded on it. References to the other black ethnic groups were woven into the discussion.

In the area that presently constitutes the Eastern Cape Province, during the latter part of the nineteenth century, Mayer (1980) noted that the school, and to some extent, the church, sustained among the Xhosa people–a latent orientation to change, ready to be activated when favourable opportunities occurred. In this population, the most frequently highlighted change in the reproductive patterns among women was a rapid growth in the incidence of extramarital childbearing and the various manifestations of this phenomenon, such as the growth in the incidence of matrifocal households and the consequent decline of the patrilineal system. Similar observations were noted among the Tswana (Schapera 1933, 1971; Krige 1936). Various explanations have been advanced for the increase in extra–marital childbirths among black women in South Africa in general.

The discussion which follows focused on the Xhosa population in conceptualizing the changes under consideration as unfolding in three distinct phases which are implied in the literature sources consulted. Such phases must, however, be understood to have the weak temporal and geographic boundaries which characterize social change. The first phase had the longest duration and was characterized by the continued absence of the concept of regulation of childbearing, the emergence of Christian exhortations for changes in sexual and marital behavioural patterns and legislative instruments which backed those exhortations. The foundation for reproduction to slip out of marriage and traditional control were laid down during this phase.

During the second phase, socio-economic circumstances emerged as a dominant force in influencing marriage patterns. Simultaneously, the social control over childbearing declined. Modern means of fertility regulation were viewed with suspicion, but growth in formal education and urban influences lay the foundations for their acceptance. Reproduction inside and outside marriage ran parallel to each other.

The third and emerging phase appears to be characterized by a further weakening of traditional controls on women's childbearing behaviour, legislative support for reproductive autonomy and a stronger governmental role in the provision of reproductive health services. Women's personal development along with their developmental role at all levels of society are emphasized in conformity to the guidelines set out in the Programme of Action set out at the 1994 Cairo Conference on Population and Development. The following section presented review of literature which provides an elaboration of these three phases.

2.3.1 The Christian Conversion and Value Confrontation Phase

As pointed out in Chapter 1, the historical contact of the black South Africans with western culture and Christian religion impacted in women's reproductive patterns in various ways. In addition to the Christian prescription of hetero-sexual monogamy in marriage, Foucault (1978) described the relation between western power and sex as a negative one, consisting of rejection, exclusion, refusal, blockage and concealment or mask. He pointed out to an insistence on rules, distinguishing between licit and illicit, permitted and forbidden in a cycle of prohibition. Foucault explains further that nothing that was not ordered in terms of generation or transfigured by it could expect sanction or protection, nor did it merit hearing. It would be driven out, denied and reduced to silence. Not only did it not exist, it had no right to exist and would be made to disappear upon its least manifestation—whether in acts or in words. In Foucault's view, through the political economy of population, there was formed a whole grid of observations regarding sex. There emerged the analysis of the modes of sexual conduct, their determination and their effects, at the boundary line of the biological and the economic domains.

Regarding sexual norms of the Xhosa, Mayer and Mayer (1974) found, in a research that included Xhosa Christians, that sexual satisfaction was viewed as a normal requirement for every adult, whether married, unmarried or widowed, provided sexual contacts were regulated to avoid infringement of inherent rights. Sexual expression was not viewed as intrinsically evil or dangerous. This outlook was contrary to the Christian perspective that exalted celibacy and grudgingly conceded to sexual expression, but only within marriage, and even then, for the purpose of procreation. Christian exhortations were also made against certain sexual norms like the practice of non-penetrative sex by youth.

For the Xhosa population, the phase of confrontation of values governing sexuality, marriage and reproduction extended from the time of capitulation to colonial rule in the 1850s to the period of growing recruitment of mine labour. It preceded the emergence of the notion of regulation of childbearing among Xhosa women but presented a variety of significant value confrontations. For instance, in examining conversion into Christianity among Xhosa society, Pauw captures the puzzling phenomenon of syncretism, when he says, "... The missionary expected them to shed all traditional Xhosa beliefs and rituals relating to ancestors, witchcraft and sorcery, divining and medicines as well as customs like traditional dancing, giving and receiving ikhazi (marriage goods) and polygyny... In the external features of social structure and culture, Western forms largely superseded those of Xhosa tradition" (Pauw 1975, 21).

For the Xhosa people, religious conversion did not imply relinquishing their traditional belief in ancestors, which, for the purposes of this discussion, formed the basis of their reproductive behaviour. As noted in the discussion of the socio-historical landmarks of the subject population in

Chapter 1, the converts lived in two somewhat conflicting "worlds", and their behaviour reflected this ambivalence. Christian religion challenged, among other things the value system which formed the basis of marital and reproductive unions, as well as the norms which governed the sexual morality of the Xhosa.

Wilson (1981) notes that new legal forms of marriage were established under Colonial Law, Roman Dutch Law and the Statutes of the Cape applied to the Ciskei, then British Kaffraria from 1860, as Ordinance 1 of British Kaffraria, and under Laws and Regulations of British Kaffraria, since 1869. The new laws made the payment of bride-wealth not a legal requirement for marriage, because of the perception that payment of bride-wealth constituted a sale of the woman. Many households also faced a decline of cattle holdings, making it difficult for young men to make bride-wealth payments. In addition, under colonial law, a marriage contract was null if coercion was proved (Wilson 1981). Wilson explains that the principle that a marriage without the consent of the bride was contrary to natural justice was widely maintained throughout colonial Africa. In corroboration of this, she cites Hunter's (1936) observation that after the annexation of Pondoland into Cape governance, girls being forced into distasteful marriages sought and were granted protection by magistrates. Irate parents on the other hand wanted to uphold their control over marriages, and Wilson (1971) cites evidence given by a Xhosa before a government commission, with insistence that *"... a thing called love"* was destroying parental control and causing illegitimacy.

Mayer and Mayer (1974), on their part, argue that in prescribing sexual purity, the Christian value system derogated the traditional norm of non-penetrative sex for young girls, viewing it as fornication. They point out that the abandonment of guidance on non-penetrative sexual intercourse opened way for full sex, since the view that sexual relations were perverse was inconsistent with the value systems of the Xhosa people and sexual incontinence for males was never internalized.

Concerning polygamy, Wilson (1971) explains that polygamy links closely with subsistence herding and cultivation, where there is ample land to allow each wife her own plot for cultivating food for her household's subsistence needs. Wilson notes further that polygamy requires particular demographic conditions where marriageable women outnumber men, as is the case after a war or due to differential survival of men and women, but more commonly where the prescribed age for marriage for men and women differs substantially, such that girls aged 16–26 are married while males in those age groups are not. She attributed the decline of polygamous unions to both religious conversions and economic decline, and noted that the decline in polygamy raised proportions of single women in the Xhosa population.

2.3.2 *The Declining Subsistence Economy and Rise of Urban Norms and Values*

This period extended from roughly the end of the Second World War to the 1970s. The distinguishing historical milestones for the second phase were a booming post-war modern sector of the economy in South Africa, which drew its labour from the faltering rural subsistence economy described by the Tomlinson Commission (Houghton 1956). Internationally, fertility regulation gained momentum during this period. The economic decline among the rural black population accelerated the pace of labour migration to urban areas, where traditional normative controls over sexual and reproductive behaviour were markedly low. The growth in education, which encompassed girls as well, contributed to the changes which appeared during this phase.

The 1953 Tomlinson Report provided a detailed account of the progressive deterioration of the subsistence economy of the rural reserves of South Africa. The economic situation of the Xhosa population declined in the classical manner in which the subsistence sector of a dual economy declines on juxtaposition with a modern economy. The decline in cattle holdings was attributed to population increase and limited grazing (Wilson 1981). Such declines, however, can often be traced to a multiplicity of causes. The exploitative relationship between the modern and the subsistence sector in a dual economy often erodes the subsistence sector and causes poverty. Wilson (1981) also notes that the Xhosa lost a substantial part of their herds in the cattle killing of 1857 during the Xhosa National Suicide[1] and they never achieved cattle holdings comparable to those of the early nineteenth century. The rinderpest also contributed enormously to the decline in cattle holdings among the Xhosa. Pearce (2000, 28) describes the rinderpest as "the microbe that shaped Africa," in a discussion which outlines the impact of the epidemic on cattle in its spread through the continent. For the Southern African region, Pearce notes that by the end of the nineteenth century, an estimated 5.5 million cattle had died, in a massive destruction of the wealth of the Xhosa people.

Wilson and Thompson (1969,) and Wilson (1971) estimate the number of cattle for the Ciskei area in the 18th and early 19th centuries at two to three times the human population, compared to 0.5 to 1 or less, times the human population in the 1970s. Wilson (1981) notes further that since the number of cattle required for a marriage did not fall appreciably and the cost of cattle in cash terms increased steadily, the difficulty of a man marrying increased. As cattle stock holdings diminished and consumption in trade goods increased, fathers were less able and willing to help their sons to

---

[1] During this historical milestone, a prophecy that the white colonizers would be blown into the ocean by a strong wind if the Xhosa population killed all their livestock and destroyed their crops came to nothing.

marry. With the tradition of raiding cattle from other chiefdoms as one of the ways of securing cattle for bride price being outlawed, wage labour became the only way of acquiring cattle. This economic decline of the Xhosa population opened way for a growing dependence on the modern sector of the South African economy, with growing reliance on migration to urban areas.

The economic changes discussed previously in this book resulted in the increase of marital age for both men and women. Wilson *et al* (1952) cite evidence in the Keiskammahoek area of the Eastern Cape, before 1890, where the average age of men at first marriage was 24.3 years. By the 1930s, it had advanced to 28.6 years, and between 1945 and 1950 it reached 30.1 years. Marital age for women in the same district advanced from 19.3 years before 1890 to 23.6 years in the 1940s. Findings from a sample of 51 informants from the Tyhume valley of the Victoria East district of the Eastern Cape province interviewed in 1972 indicated that average age of marriage was 27 years for males and 20 for women (Raum and De Jager1972). Wilson (1981) explains that the gap in marriage age of men and women was around five to seven years and increasing. The situation indicated the existence at any time of larger numbers of marriageable women than men. The decline in polygamy meant that nearly a fifth of women could not marry. Wilson also noted high male mortality and a high incidence of widowhood in Keiskammahoek district in 1950 and in the Victoria East and Middledrift districts of the Eastern Cape in the 1960s. Such mortality increased the proportions of single women at any given time.

Wilson (1971) explained that acute social difficulties arise if polygamy diminishes rapidly, whether for economic or religious reasons, and a marked difference in the marriage age of men and women or in their survival rate remains. Mayer (1980) observed that during this period, the temptation to polygamy was negligible, and that even among the "red people," few Xhosa had more than one wife. He argued that extra-marital relations constituted a greater enemy of Christian sexual morality than polygamy, adding that the average Xhosa Christian took care to conceal his sins from church authorities, and that discretion became an important notion for the Xhosa "school people."

From early colonial years, the expansion of education became another significant factor in the evolution of the women's reproductive behaviour. In the Tyhume valley of the Victoria East district of the Eastern Cape Province, Backhouse (1844, cited by Wilson 1971) reported 75 females and 54 males in school, and that girls soon made teachers and from 1903 onwards girls began training as nurses. Wilson (1971) describes this as an indication that there was no great pressure on women to get married immediately after puberty. Girls with various levels of schooling entered both rural and urban employment markets, making incomes which gave them economic independence, a factor which was inconsistent with the female dependency that has been inherent in patriarchal systems.

Finally, another important development during this phase was that the decline of the rural economy opened way for migration of rural working age populations to urban areas and exposure of many rural people to the urban environment which lacked the traditional normative constraints to sexual and reproductive behaviour. Mayer and Mayer (1961) documented the different reactions of the "red people" and the "school people" who went to East London from the rural districts surrounding it. Concubinage, which is described by Wilson (1981) as a long-term relationship between a woman and a man which is not recognized as a legal marriage, was a prominent feature observed by the Meyers among black migrants in East London.

With regard to reproduction from such concubinage, Jones (1992) documents the movements of children of migrant parents between the various urban centres of South Africa and rural relatives, with grand-parents frequently called upon to be surrogate parents in the case of out-of-wedlock children, in accordance with custom. With the decline of the subsistence economy, the economic position of rural grand-parents was often precarious, and this made it difficult for them to discharge their traditional responsibility of fostering children placed in their care by unmarried daughters, particularly where a string of such births kept coming from the daughter, with minimal contribution for their maintenance. Jones' ethnographic study (1992) documents the childbearing and parenting strategies among migrants in different cities, the child fostering networks provided by rural communities of origin for the migrants, and the precarious existence and identity problems which attended the lives of children who grow under such circumstances.

Wilson (1981) explains that under traditional law, children of an unmarried mother belong to her father or brother, and that the common pattern in rural areas has been that such children are left in the girl's parents' or brother's homestead, while the mother sought work to support them. She adds that since rural communities have ceased to be self-supporting in food, children have become a liability rather than an asset, and that medical evidence shows that it is illegitimate children who suffer most from malnutrition.

The women's perspective on these developments warrants attention. In a qualitative study of South African Tswana women in Phokeng, whose reproductive years spanned the period between 1900 and 1983, Bozzoli and Nkotsoe (1991) found that by the women's own standards of decency, as opposed to those of their patriarchal controllers, it was acceptable to have several children by a boyfriend before marriage, provided one subsequently married the father of the children. Bozzoli and Nkotsoe also found that for the 15 women for whom the fullest information was available, the average age at marriage was as high as 27 years, and the highest age was 43 years. But this marital age had no bearing at all on their reproductive age, which frequently was younger than the marital age. From this exposition, it, therefore, emerges that marital age has a limited relationship to the onset of childbearing amongst black South African women.

A perspective cited by Mayer and Mayer (1961) which emanated from Xhosa women in their East London study is that decency requires that a woman should try as far as possible to keep the affections of her children's father, because to bear illegitimate children to more than one man is unworthy of a self-respecting woman. Mayer and Mayer further note that Xhosa women want their children to have the same decency on the father's side, because children of different fathers will have different customs and will be more likely to quarrel. They also note the practical reality that a new lover may dislike the children of his predecessor. Mayer and Mayer concluded that these reasons make mothers of illegitimate children ready to humble themselves towards the father of their children in order to prolong the relationship.

The 1968 United Nations Conference held in Teheran expounded the rights of couples to information and services to enable them to have the desired number of children. In South Africa, the Family Planning Programme came about in 1975. At the ground level, however, particularly in rural areas, regulating childbearing remained a vaguely understood, foreign and objectionable notion. Nevertheless, it was there, and economic and educational developments had yet to strengthen the substratum for it to attract the attention of women.

2.3.3 Matrilineal Consolidation, Childbirth Regulation and AIDS Prevention

In their 2004 evaluation of achievements made 10 years after the 1994 International Conference on Population and Development, Ethelston *et al.* (2004) argue that despite some improvements, tremendous challenges remain. They estimate that more than 3.5 million women worldwide die of reproductive health-related causes, and that 99 per cent of such deaths still take place in developing countries. They point out that reproductive illnesses weaken or kill people during their most economically productive years, exacting a financial toll to individuals and families as well as undermining economic development. They view women's ability to manage their fertility as critical to gender equality and poverty reduction, because smaller family size supports savings and investment. They place the onus of taking on controversial issues such as youth services and abortion at the doorstep of governments and donors, and urge for the support of progressive legislation by civil society organizations, especially non-governmental organisations.

In the South African context, the third phase of changes in the reproductive behaviour of black women in South Africa can be described as a consolidation of growth in regulation of childbirth, a growing acceptance of the matrilineal household as an enduring feature of South African society, and efforts to control the spread of AIDS. This phase roughly extends from the mid of the second half of the 20th century to early 21st century. The South African National Family Planning Programme's Education, Information and Communication campaigns along with an extensive service network in the 1980s and 1990s elicited a response across all communities in South Africa. For the black population, growing rural poverty weakened the traditional accommodative capacity of families to shoulder the responsibility of illegitimate children, and female-headed households became a reality whose plight challenged society and the state. The growth in women's education and their participation in the labour market, along with the growing cost of children with expanding education may have contributed to changes in the family-formation aspirations of women. The emergence of AIDS whose preventive strategies include barrier methods and sexual abstinence may also be contributing to the emerging scenario of reproductive behaviour at all levels.

Various national surveys have been conducted to map out the changes in aspects of women's reproductive behaviour. Next were reviewed literature on findings derived from the analyses of data from three such surveys: 1) the 1993 Project Statistics on Living Standards and Development (PSLSD) which was conducted by the Southern African Labour Development Research Unit (SALDRU), 2) the Demographic and Health Survey (SADHS) 1987–89) conducted by the Human Sciences Research Council, and 3) the SADHS (1998) which was done jointly by the Department of Health, Macro International, the Medical Research Council.

Mencarini (1999) made an analysis of the 1993 PSLSD interview data from 8,848 South African households with a total of 10,453 women of reproductive age. Although the research was directed at analyzing infant mortality dynamics, it incorporated dynamics on selected aspects of women's reproductive behaviour, which are relevant to this research, namely mean age at first childbirth, total fertility rates and estimates of legitimate and illegitimate fertility. Only the findings which pertain to the black population were reported on in this discussion. Mencarini noted that the picture of fertility drawn by PSLSD for the black population was scarcely linked to marriage and reflected a progressive reduction, with a mean age of first birth of about 22 years. The summarized findings are presented in Table 2. 1.

Table 2. 1 Estimates of fertility, mean age at birth and legitimacy of births in the black population of South Africa, 1993

Variables	Estimates
TFR 1984-8	4.8
TFR 1989-93	3.85
Mean age at birth for all parities 1984-88	30.3
Mean age at birth for all parities 1989-93	29.1
Mean age at first birth	21.9
Legitimate TFR 1989-93	4.1
Illegitimate TFR 1989-93	2.7

SOURCE: Mencarini (1999, 114)

From a preliminary univariate analysis of these data, Mencarini found that the most important factors for lower relative fertility for women of all population groups in South Africa seemed to be higher education, urban residence and higher economic standard of living.

Du Plessis (1999) made comparisons of women's fertility preferences from the findings of the 1987–89 and 1998 Demographic and Health Surveys that have been used in this research and had a 10-year time gap between them. Both surveys included questions aimed at establishing the number of children considered ideal, the preferred spacing between births and whether respondents wanted more children.

For the black women aged 25–44, the 1987–9 SADHS found a mean age at first birth of 20.3. Between the two surveys, non-numeric responses to the question on ideal family size decreased from 18.4 to 1.6 per cent. Du Plessis explains the significance of numeric and non-numeric responses to questions on family size by citing Coale's theoretical preconditions (1986) for fertility decline. These are that people should develop a calculated numerical notion about family size, that they should perceive the advantages of family limitation, and that they should have the resources to do so. The differences in ideal number of children given by black women by age category at the two surveys are shown in Table 2.2 and reflect a decline in perceived ideal number of children across all age groups.

Table 2.2. Mean ideal number of children for black South African women, 1989 and 1998

	Women's age groupings							Total
	15–19	20–24	25–29	30–34	35–39	40–44	45–49	
1989 SADHS	2.9	3.1	3.3	3.8	4.1	4.4	4.6	4.6
1998 SADHS	2.2	2.5	2.8	3.2	3.6	3.7	4.2	3.0
1998 SADHS (rural)	2.4	2.7	3.2	3.7	4.1	4.2	4.9	3.3
1998 SADHS (urban)	2.0	2.2	2.5	2.8	3.1	3.3	3.5	2.7

SOURCE: Du Plessis (1999).

Analysis of data in Table 2.2 showed that the reproductive changes occurring amongst the black rural populations of South Africa lag behind those occurring amongst the black urban populations. However, there may also be regional difference across the various rural populations. The changes taking place are also noticeable between successive age cohorts. The latter observation indicates rapid changes which reflect themselves even between cohorts with five-year age differences.

Kaufman de Wet and Stadler (2000) noted that, in contrast to many other settings, South Africa's practice of allowing teenage mothers to return to school once they have given birth provides them with an opportunity that produces a long delay before the birth of a second child. Also Mfono (2002) found from focus group discussions that after the first premarital childbirth, women face strong pressure, both from their peers and from wider society, against having a second birth before marriage.

2.4 The Salient Aspects Highlighted in the Reviewed Literature Sources

The literature sources reviewed depict the history of movement of societies from traditional methods of regulation of women's reproduction to technological regulation, with human rights, health and demographic motivation providing the dominant motivations at different points in time. The Programme of Action that was mooted at the 1994 Cairo Conference on Population and Development highlighted the human rights, health considerations along with women's empowerment in governmental pursuit of population and developmental objectives.

Where African reproductive traditions are concerned, the literature sources reviewed present a scenario of reproduction that was dominated by clan survival goals which made women reproductive objects, required large progeny and were strongly disposed towards male progeny. Polygamy served these clan survival requirements, and the biological phenomenon of reproduction was subject to an economic transaction, the transfer of bride-wealth to the woman's family.

For the South African black population, the literature sources reviewed reveal that bride wealth transactions progressively faced insurmountable economic difficulties over time, and this, along with other factors, contributed to unprecedented increases in marital age, as well as to non-marital childbearing. Western influences on reproductive norms, rapid social change, women's education and participation in the modern economic sector are challenging the black society's clan survival goals and putting women's health and personal welfare ahead of them. Rural women however lag behind their urban counterparts in these achievements, and this may well be one of the factors underlying rural poverty in South Africa. The empowering strategies for women set out in the 1994 Programme of Action appear to have more relevance for rural women.

CHAPTER 3

DESIGN AND METHODOLOGY OF THE RESEARCH

The behavioural patterns this research focused on can be subsumed under three broad categories, namely: 1) childbearing age patterns and incidence amongst childbearing age women in the subject population, 2) the various methods used in regulating childbirths and the patterns of their use, and 3) the marital and provincial variations of these patterns. Under childbearing, the behavioural variables considered were the changes over the research period in median ages at onset and at progression up to the fifth childbirth, as well changes in the number of children ever born to child-bearing age women. Secondly, the changes in age and marital patterns of use of the various methods of regulation of childbirths were analyzed, as well as the birth order stages during which the various methods were used. Thirdly, the changes in the variables considered were analyzed and compared by marital status of women and by the various provinces included in the research, and also compared to those observed in African countries and elsewhere.

3.1 Research Design and Methodology

The research was designed as a longitudinal, descriptive, quantitative and inter-cohort comparative analysis of secondary data from two national surveys—the 1987–89 and 1998 SADHS, as well as data from 2004 reproductive health service records. An empirical approach was thus used in quantifying and comparing childbearing behaviour amongst rural black women in five provinces over a period of 17 years. The design aimed at determining both the direction and the pace of the changes considered, as well as geographic differences.

The design focused firstly on the childbearing patterns of samples of reproductive age women selected for the three time periods under consideration. Descriptions and comparisons then moved on to fertility regulation patterns by contraception, voluntary sterilizations and pregnancy terminations. Finally, comparisons of childbearing patterns and its regulation were made for women who described themselves as married and those who described themselves as single at the time of the survey or records data collection. Five-year age cohorts were used to determine the pace of changes in the variables considered. The 1987–89 SADHS provided the baseline data against which the changes in 1998 and 2004 were considered.

3.1.1 The Data Sources

Electronic data sets of the 1987–89 and 1998 South African Demographic and Health Surveys were obtained from the South African Data Archives. Detailed information on the sampling methods, data collection and other methodological approaches used during these two surveys is contained on Annexures 1 and 2. From these national surveys, data on reproductive patterns of rural women from the selected provinces was extracted and analyzed for the variables included in this research for the first two time periods of the research.

For 2004, data was collected from reproductive health service records at selected rural hospitals. The 2004 service records used include: maternity registers, contraception registers, surgical procedures registers, and pregnancy terminations registers for data on childbirths, contraception, surgical sterilizations and pregnancy terminations, respectively. The data from registers on each of these aspects was supplemented with data from patients' service records whenever information was inadequate. All these records are statutory requirements for the relevant services. They are, however, confidential and are only accessible for research through official written authorization. The initial step for this research therefore consisted of securing such authorization, as well as discussions with service providers to elicit their recommendations on the use of the relevant records.

For the 2004 service records data, it was also necessary to establish the approximate proportion of rural women who used the relevant reproductive health services in recent years. From the 1995 October Household Survey, it was established that 82 per cent of black rural women had their last childbirth either in a hospital or clinic. The same survey revealed that 89 per cent of black households made use of public health facilities when they need care (Statistics South Africa 1995). The rural hospital records were thus considered as reflecting a reasonable picture of rural women's reproductive behaviour.

From the information available in the maternity registers, this research selected data on age, marital status, order of present birth and number of previous births of each woman in the sample drawn from the population of women who used the hospital maternity ward in 2004. From the contraception client record cards, data on age, occupation, marital status, and number of previous child-births were recorded for each case that was included in the sample. Sterilization records distinguish between voluntary and involuntary or medically indicated sterilizations and thus made the selection of voluntary sterilization clients possible. From these records, this research selected data on age, marital status, and number of previous births of each client who had a voluntary sterilization. From the register of requests for pregnancy terminations for the year 2004, the ages and previous births to clients who successfully requested this procedure were obtained.

3.1.2 Data Collection Instruments

Questionnaires (Annexures 1 and 2) were used for the two surveys. Data collection sheets were compiled for records data collection on the four aspects of reproductive behaviour included in this research.

Each data collection sheet has two columns, which identify each case by the hospital record number and by a case number allocated to it in this research. No client names were included in these sheets to protect the confidentiality of the clients. The hospital record number was included for tracing any case records when that was necessary for confirmation of data collected. Except for the first two columns, the data collection record sheets differed according to the data content they were designed to collect, and such content is discussed below.

i.   Data Sheet A was designed to collect maternity data and, besides the two identifying columns, it has columns on age, marital status, order of present birth, and number of previous births or parity;

ii. Data Sheets B were designed to collect data on sterilization (B1), pregnancy terminations (B2) and contraception (B3). In addition to the two identifying columns, Data Sheet B1 has columns on age, marital status, number of previous births and voluntary or involuntary nature of the sterilization. In addition to the two identifying columns, Data Sheet B2 has columns on age, and the number of previous childbirths. In addition to the two identifying columns, Data Sheet B3 has columns on age, marital status, the number of previous births and clients' occupation.

3.1.3 Sampling Techniques

The 1987–9 survey used random cluster sampling nationally to select females of reproductive age who had already given birth or were married or were exposed to conception. This sampling approach had a bias that favoured women in marital or more or less stable sexual unions. The 1998 survey, on the other hand, used stratified sampling for a broader canvassing of women in their reproductive ages, that is, 15–49 years, irrespective of their marital status or nature of sexual union, hence the larger representation of women who were never married. The 2004 data from service records was based on women who used the reproductive health services in 2004, irrespective of marital category.

For the 2004 data on births, 10 per cent samples were selected by systematic random sampling from the universe of childbirths recorded for that year. These samples provided a spread of cases over 12 months for 2004, and the sample sizes varied from hospital to hospital. The total rural sample for analysis of childbirth patterns consisted of 787 cases, of whom 60 per cent were never married, 16 per cent were currently married and 24 per cent were either divorced, widowed, living together or with no marital status information.

For 2004 family planning data, 20 per cent systematic random samples of case records of service users at each of the hospitals were selected from the total of service users for 2004. The total sample on family planning client data consisted of 574 cases. Fairly large samples of maternity and family planning records data were considered justifiable because the data was to be subdivided by marital status, age cohorts and provinces. It was considered necessary to have initial sample sizes, which would, when sub-divided, still provide plausible scenarios. Tables 3.1 to 3.4 reflect the size and marital composition of rural women on which the analyses on childbearing, contraception, sterilization and pregnancy terminations were based for each of the years considered.

Table 3.1 Size and marital status of rural women samples used for   childbearing analyses

Marital status	Size or proportion (in %)		
	1987–89	1998	2004
Never married	25	46	60
Currently married	55	45	16
Other*	20	9	24
Total number	9976	3138	787

* Divorced, widowed or living together.

Table 3.2. Size and marital status of rural women samples used for **analyses** of contraception

Marital status	Size or proportion (in %)		
	1987–89	1998	2004
Never married	20	51	Na*
Currently married	59	33	na
Other**	21	16	na
Total number	6405	1962	1051

*na= not available   ** Divorced, widowed or living together.

Because of their smaller universes, surgical sterilization and pregnancy termination cases for 2004 were all included in the research. The sample sizes used for these analyses are reflected on Tables 3.3 and 3.4.

Table 3.3. Size and marital status of rural women samples used for sterilization analyses

Marital status	Size or proportion (in %)		
	1987–89	1998	2004
Never married	5	11	26
Currently married	77	64	74
Other*	18	25	0
Total number	199	184	53

* Divorced, widowed or living together.

Table 3.4. Size of rural women samples used for pregnancy termination analyses

	Size in year considered		
	1987–89	1998	2004
Number	na	523	198

3.1.4 Data Processing and Analysis

For the demographic and health surveys data, the STATA software programme was used to extract data on rural women by age and by province, and statistics on the selected variables were generated and set out in descriptive tables and graphs for the time periods of the research. The 2004 data from the data sheets was entered into spreadsheet files and descriptive tables and graphs matching those derived from the survey data were generated. From this combination, a longitudinal scenario on each of the variables included in the research was derived on the overall trends amongst rural women during the three periods considered, as well as for single and married women, for the different provinces and for the various age cohorts of rural women. Longitudinal scenarios of the unfolding of the different behavioural variables thus emerged for interpretation and discussion.

3.2 The Design and Methodological Constraints of this Research

The design and methodological limitations that are inherent in this research are now considered, along with the strategies that were used to address them. Most of the constraints arise from the use of secondary data. Concerning the use of such data, Glenn (1977) comments that data collected at different times may not be comparable, because of changes in the data collection instruments and approaches used. In this particular research, the 1987–9 data set used females of reproductive age who had already given birth or who were married or exposed to pregnancy as the sampling frame. That analysis thus specifically focused on sexually active women. The 1998 data set, on the other hand, was drawn from women of reproductive age, irrespective of their marital status or being sexually active. As a result it contained large proportions of women who responded that they were not sexually active. Finally, the 2004 data set consisted of clients who had used reproductive health services in 2004, whether for childbirth, regulation of childbirths by contraception, sterilization or pregnancy termination. The 2004 sampling frame for family planning also differed from the sampling frames of the two earlier surveys because some family planning users were not necessarily sexually active, but used contraception to prevent conception in the event of rape. The variations in sampling frames had the potential of generating findings that are not comparable across the time periods considered in the research.

This shortcoming suggests a weakening of the comparative analysis of percentages of women using contraception, but has no impact on contraceptive use patterns estimated by birth order. Data on childbearing, sterilizations and pregnancy terminations were not vulnerable to the discrepancies in the sampling techniques used, since they pertained to women who had gone through these reproductive behavioural events.

Other limitations of secondary data sources cited by Glenn are that informants may be reluctant to impart information details they consider as sensitive, 'over-report' socially approved behaviour and attitudes and underreport disapproved behaviour and attitudes. In this research, it is possible that reproductive health clients may have hidden information which would elicit criticism from health care workers. The reporting of marital status is potentially vulnerable, because of varying perceptions on the acceptability of reproductive health service use by single women, particularly adolescents. This may have been the case particularly during the time of the 1987–89 SADHS, when the government and South African society were ambivalent on the issue of adolescent contraceptive use. Such ambivalence had, however, probably declined at the time of the 1998 SADHS because of the governmental endorsement of reproductive health service access to all women of reproductive ages.

In his analyses of constraints imposed by secondary data on cohort analyses, Glenn (1977) pointed to the necessity of data spanning long periods of 20 or more years, which in turn prescribes the utilizing of available data that was originally collected for other purposes. This constraint restricts the selection of dependent variables to what the available data may dictate, and this fact had relevance for the present study. Firstly it determined how far back the study could go, because the 1987–9 data was from the oldest national survey that contained most of the variables required for this research. Data availability on pregnancy terminations could only date back to the 1998 survey, the only national survey conducted after pregnancy terminations were legalized. The time frame of the research and selection of variables was, therefore, dictated by these constraints on variable selection and the time period for consideration.

Data for the 2004 analyses was difficult to obtain, and the initial plan of using data from five provinces had to be abandoned. Accessing health records data was a complicated process that required prolonged engagement with the provincial governmental bureaucracy that has been put in place to protect records data. Such engagement proved to be very time consuming, and only three of the originally intended five provinces had provided the requisite access to their records data before the decision had to be made to proceed with data analysis in reasonable time to meet the deadlines set for this research.

The quality of 2004 records data for research purposes was found to vary enormously across the institutions included in the research. This must be understood against the reality that the primary purpose of reproductive records data collection is service provision. Thus, marital status, for instance, which is a socio-demographic characteristic, is often missing from some reproductive health forms, even in those in which space is provided for it. It has to be conceded that, from a health perspective, age and other aspects are much more important. It is also probable that health service providers do not consider service records as future research data sources. Staff shortages were highlighted at one of the centres as critically affecting the compiling of records. The particular centre's records were quite below the standard of the others included in the research, and staff members often had to be appealed to for help in making sense of what was recorded. On the other hand, one of the centres included in the research had an extremely well-organized records compiling and filing system which made data collection convenient and much less time consuming, indicating records data to be a viable research option.

The high prevalence of AIDS in the research context warrants analytic attention to its specific impact on reproductive behavioural patterns considered. The survey data, however, indicated a very low incidence of condom use amongst the respondents, and the records data used in 2004 did not have data on condom use. The methodological approach used thus excludes analysis of conformity to AIDS prevention strategies, even though it can be assumed that AIDS prevalence most likely has a significant impact on the emerging reproductive patterns.

3.3 How Ethical Considerations were Taken into Account in this Research

Ethical constraints constitute a specific category in research and always warrant mention. In this research, anonymity of individual clients was observed in the use of records data. Such anonymity also applied to the rural hospitals from which data was collected. Because the research design included provincial comparisons the trends in the various provinces were reported on. The provincial reproductive service conditions that had been highlighted in other provincial and local studies were also reported on.

CHAPTER 4
RESEARCH FINDINGS

The following research findings reflected firstly the changes in the childbearing patterns of the subject population of rural women, focusing on the age patterns at onset and during childbearing progression, as well as the number of childbirths per woman. The differences between married and single women on these aspects, as well as the variations of the trends between the provinces included in the research were also encompassed. Next, the changes in the patterns of fertility regulation by contraception, sterilizations and pregnancy terminations were reported on in that same sequence, along with the provincial variations in these trends and between the national and the rural scenarios.

4.1 Changes in Rural Women's Childbearing Patterns

4.1.1 Changes in the Age Patterns of Onset and Progression of Childbearing

Figure 4.1 Changes in Median Childbearing Ages, 1987–89, 1998 and 2004

The 2004 data reflected an upward shift in childbearing ages, compared to the 1987–89 and 1998 data, which reflected remarkably similar childbearing onset and progression age childbearing patterns, despite a 10–year time gap between them. The median age at onset of childbearing was 19 years during the two Demographic and Health Surveys, but had shifted upwards to 20 years in 2004 (see Figure 4.1). This upward shift in the median age at onset of childbearing was, however, small compared to the overall upward shift in child-bearing progression ages reflected by the 2004 data, which suggested wider spacing of births subsequent to the first birth among rural women in recent years.

While the median age at onset of childbearing over the three periods considered reflected a small upward shift, the median age gap between the first and second births increased from an initial four-year time span in 1987–89 and 1998 to a seven-year time span in 2004. Subsequent childbirths reflected less wide spacing in the 2004 data than the second birth, but overall, childbearing progression shifted towards older ages. The small change in the age of childbearing onset was subjected to further analysis to confirm its authenticity, in consideration of the variety of implications of childbearing that occurs among the adolescent or under-20 age group.

Detailed analysis of childbearing onset indicated that a consistent directional age trend on the age of childbearing onset has yet to emerge amongst the populations considered. The constitution of the three samples also possibly influenced the elicited pattern. Figure 4.2 for, instance, reflects that a higher percentage of first childbirths—nearly 54 per cent, occurred to women under 20 years in 1998 compared to the 1987–9 percentage of 49. Although this trend was reversed by a small margin to 53 per cent in 2004, the percentage of first childbirths to adolescent women remained higher than it was in 1987–9. Also childbearing onset amongst the 20–24 year age cohort increased by three per cent from 38 per cent in 2004 in comparison to 35 per cent in 1998, confirming the upward shift in age at onset of childbearing presented in Figure 4.1. The older age cohorts, however, reflected a consistently lower than 10 per cent contribution to first childbirths.

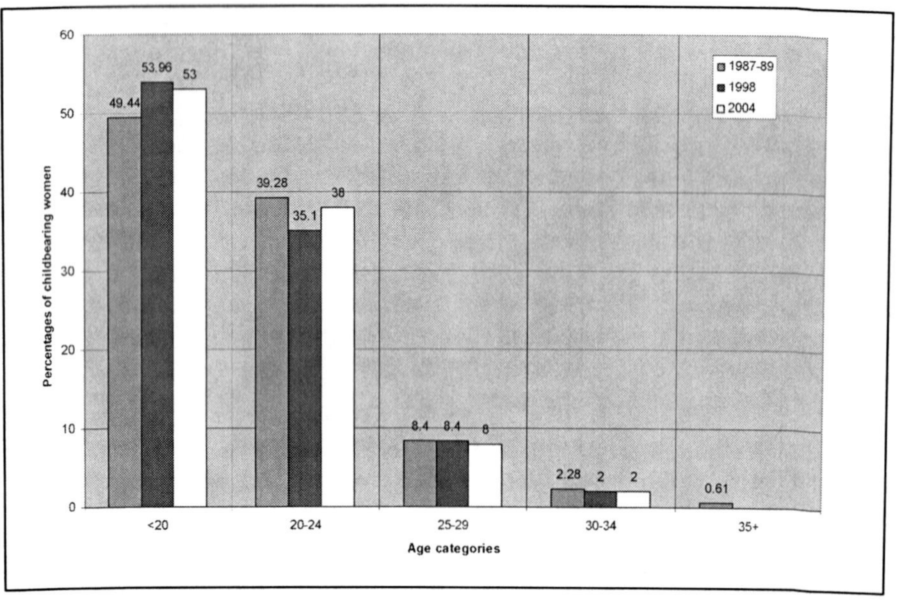

Figure 4.2 Aggregate Changes in Age at Childbearing Onset, 1987–89, 1998, 2004.

4.1.2 National and Provincial Age Variations in Childbearing Onset among Rural Women

Table 4.1 National and provincial variations in black rural women's childbearing onset ages*

Provinces	Median ages 1987–89	Median ages 1998	Median ages 2004
Nationally	20 (20.48)	19 (20.05)	na
All rural women	19 (19.96)	19 (19.87)	19 (20.04)
Eastern Cape	20 (20.88)	19 (19.95)	19 (19.65)
Limpopo	19 (19.74)	19 (19.87)	na
KwaZulu-Natal	21 (21.73	19 (19.84)	22 (23.5)
Mpumalanga	18 (18.70)	18 (18.53)	20 (20.52)
North West	20 (19.8)	19 (19.63)	na

*Mean ages in brackets

Analysis of childbearing onset by province indicated that a decrease in ages of women at childbearing onset in the period 1987–89 and 1998 occurred across four of the provinces included in this research. The decline in median age at onset of childbearing impacted on both the national trend and the overall trend among rural women. KwaZulu-Natal witnessed the highest median ages at onset of childbearing in 1987–9 and 2004, and these figures make the 1998 median problematic, with its mean that is close to 20 years. This scenario suggests a higher age at onset of childbearing in that province than the national trend. The Mpumalanga Province conversely reflected the youngest ages at onset of childbearing during the first two periods, even though the median age reflected an upward trend in 2004. The Eastern Cape Province had a consistent fall in age at first childbirth over the three time periods considered. The Limpopo province had a modest increase in the median age at childbearing onset between 1987–89 and 1998, while the North-West reflected a modest fall in median age. For 2004, data was not available for these two provinces. In 2004, reversal of the trend towards early childbearing onset was noted in both the KwaZulu-Natal and the Mpumalanga Provinces.

4.1.3 Age at Onset of Childbearing by Women's Marital Status

Table 4.2. Median ages at childbearing onset by women's marital status*

Year	Median ages at childbearing onset	
	Never married	Ever married
1987–89	20 (20.33)	19 (19.78)
1998	19 (19.28)	20 (20.24)
2004	19 (20.25)	20 (21.8)

* Mean ages in brackets.

Analysis of childbearing onset by marital status of women indicated a progressive increase in the age at onset of childbearing amongst married women. Among unmarried women, the median age at onset of childbearing dropped by one year between 1987–89 and 1998 and has remained at that level in 2004 (Table 4.2) This creates a scenario in which the ages at onset of childbearing between married and single women reflect contrasting directional patterns, hence the marginal changes in overall age at onset of childbearing reflected in Figure 4.1. As presented in Table 4.2, also the onset of childbearing amongst unmarried women began later than amongst married women in 1987–89, but this pattern was reversed, and the data for 1998 and 2004 reflected earlier onset of childbearing among rural single women than amongst their married counterparts.

4.1.4 The Birth Order Proportions of Women of Childbearing Age

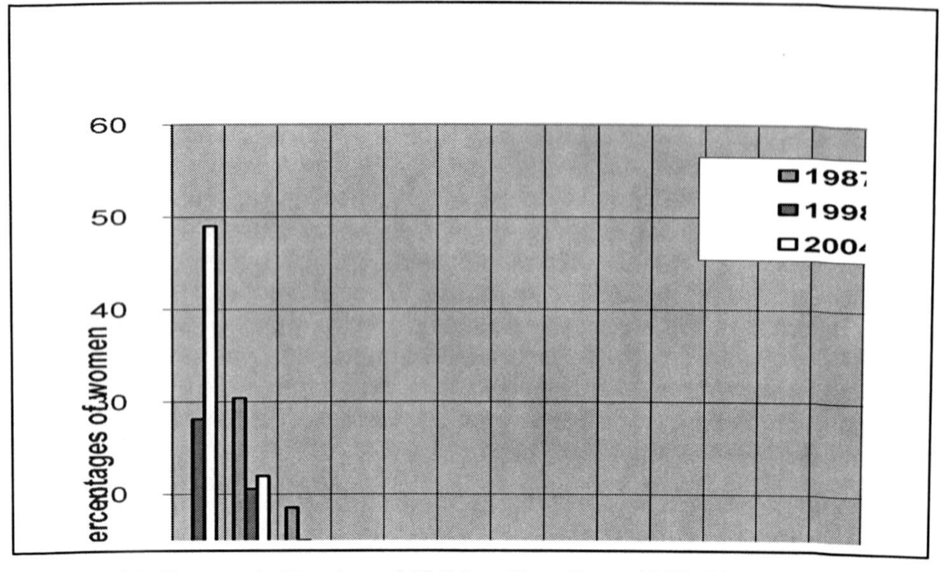

Figure 4.3 Changes in Number of Children Ever Born, 1987–89, 1998, 2004

Grouping childbearing age women by current birth order during the three time periods indicated a progressive increase in the proportion of women with no previous childbirths, with this group containing the largest proportions of women in 1998 and 2004. The proportion of women with first births on the other hand decreased in 1998 compared to what it was in 1987-9, but increased modestly in 2004. For subsequent birth orders, a pattern of progressive decline in the proportions of women with higher order births during the three time periods was noted. This decline was steeper for the period between 1998 and 2004, compared to the period between 1987–89 and 1998 (Figure 4.3).

4.1.5 Changes in the Mean CEB to Rural Childbearing Age Women

Where the mean number of children ever born (CEB) to all women of childbearing age is concerned, there has been a decline from a mean of 2.55 in 1987–89 to 1.95 in 1998 and to 1.18 in 2004. The changes in the mean CEB for rural black women, however, varied across provinces, mostly falling above the national trend for this group (Table 4.3).

Table 4.3. Mean number of CEB to rural women, 1987–9, 1998 and 2004

	Mean CEB/year (in number)		
	1987–9	1998	2004
Nationally	2.55	1.95	na
Rural blacks	2.66	2.005	1.18
Eastern Cape	2.98	2.33	2.49
Limpopo	2.58	1.97	na
KwaZulu-Natal	2.12	2.49	1.14
Mpumalanga	2.71	2.15	2.01
North West	2.35	1.93	na

Although the mean number of children even born to black rural women reflected a progressive decline during the three periods compared, the Eastern Cape rural women had the highest mean number of births in 1987–89 and 2004, and their mean CEB was second only to that of KwaZulu-

Natal women in 1998 (Table 4.3). The KwaZulu-Natal mean CEB went from being the lowest in 1987–89 to being the highest for all provinces 1998, but dropped dramatically in 2004. In the Mpumalanga Province, mean number of CEB to rural women of childbearing age reflected a consistent decline during the periods considered. The North West Province consistently had a mean that was the lowest among the provinces compared in 1987–89 and 1998, and was also lower than the national mean for the two periods. The Limpopo Province's mean remained slightly above the national mean for 1987–89 and 1998, falling along with it below two in 1998. Data for Limpopo and North West provinces and also the national level data were not available for 2004 to determine the more recent trend in mean CEB (Table 4.3).

4.1.6 Marital Variations in Mean CEB amongst Rural Black Women

The analysis of CEB by women's marital status indicated contrasting directional trends. While single women reflected a consistent decline in the mean number of CEB over the period considered in the analysis, married women reflected an increase in this mean in 1998, which was sustained in 2004 (Table 4.4).

Table 4.4. Mean number of CEB by marital status of women

Year	Mean CEB (number)	
	Never married	Ever married
1987–89	1 (1.4)	2 (2.93)
1998	.87 (0)	3 (3.06)
2004	.71 (0)	3 (2.9)

4.2 Findings on Patterns of Contraception

The analyses reported on in this section focused first on the patterns of contraception, next on patterns of use of surgical sterilization, and finally on use of pregnancy terminations. The analyses of contraception focused on the unfolding age patterns of contraception, the previous childbirths of current users of contraceptives, and the marital and provincial patterns of timing of contraceptive use in relation to childbearing onset. The last section focused on how rural women chose among the various methods of contraception available to them, including surgical sterilizations and pregnancy terminations, and these choices are compared both by marital status and by provinces.

4.2.1 *The Age Dynamics of Current Contraceptive Use*

Table 4.5. Age cohort composition changes among current contraceptive users

Age cohort	composition (%) in years considered		
	1987–89	1998	2004
< 20	14	18	11
20–24	25	25	29
25–29	15	19	28
30–34	13	15	17
35–39	11	14	9
40–44	9	6	5
45–49	13	3	1
	100	100	100
Number	6405	1962	1051

As reflected in Table 4.5, current contraceptive use was the highest by the 20–24 years age cohort, followed by the 25–29 years age cohort during the time periods compared. The under-20 years and the 30–34 years age cohorts occupied a second position in prominence, while the 40–44 and 45–49 years age cohorts reflected progressive declines in current contraceptive use. Current use of contraception among the under-20 years age group increased between 1987–89 and 1998 but decreased between 1998 and 2004. This trend was observed also among the 35–39 years age cohorts (Table 4.5).

4.2.2 *Previous Childbirths Among Current Contraceptive Users*

Contraceptive use before childbearing onset increased in 1998 from its 1987–9 level, suggesting that increasing proportions of childbearing age women desired to delay childbearing onset. This pattern of delaying childbearing onset dropped by more than 25 per cent in 2004, and was replaced by the highest rate of contraception after the first childbirth, which reached a peak of close to 45 per cent of current contraceptive users. That pattern of contraception shifted childbearing postponement from the first to the second childbirths. Although the 1998 contraceptive users increased slightly after the second births, the percentages of women who used contraception after the second and subsequent births progressively declined during all the periods considered (Figure 4.4).

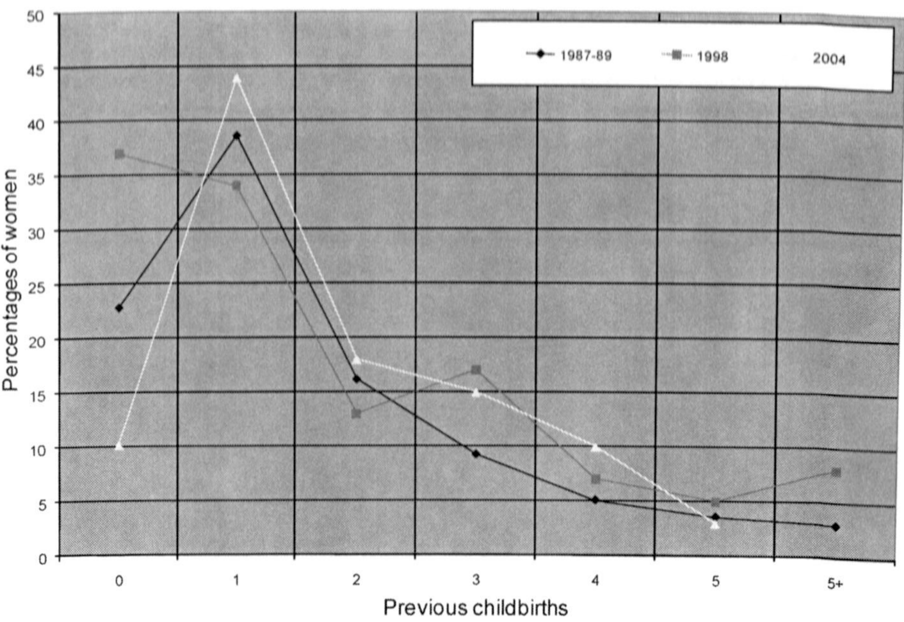

Figure 4.4. Previous Childbirths amongst Rural Current Contraceptive Users, During 1987–89, 1998, and 2004

4.2.3 Provincial Variations in Contraception in Relation to Childbearing Onset

Changes in the use of contraception before the onset of childbearing reflected variations both nationally and across the provinces considered. Figure 4.5, the North West Province had the largest increase in percentages of rural women who used contraception before childbearing onset between 1987–9 and 1998. This increase was larger than the national increase. This directional pattern was reflected also by the aggregate data for rural black women, but is modest in the Eastern Cape and Mpumalanga Provinces. KwaZulu-Natal and Limpopo Provinces on the other hand reflected a contrary trend, with reductions in use of contraception before onset of childbearing.

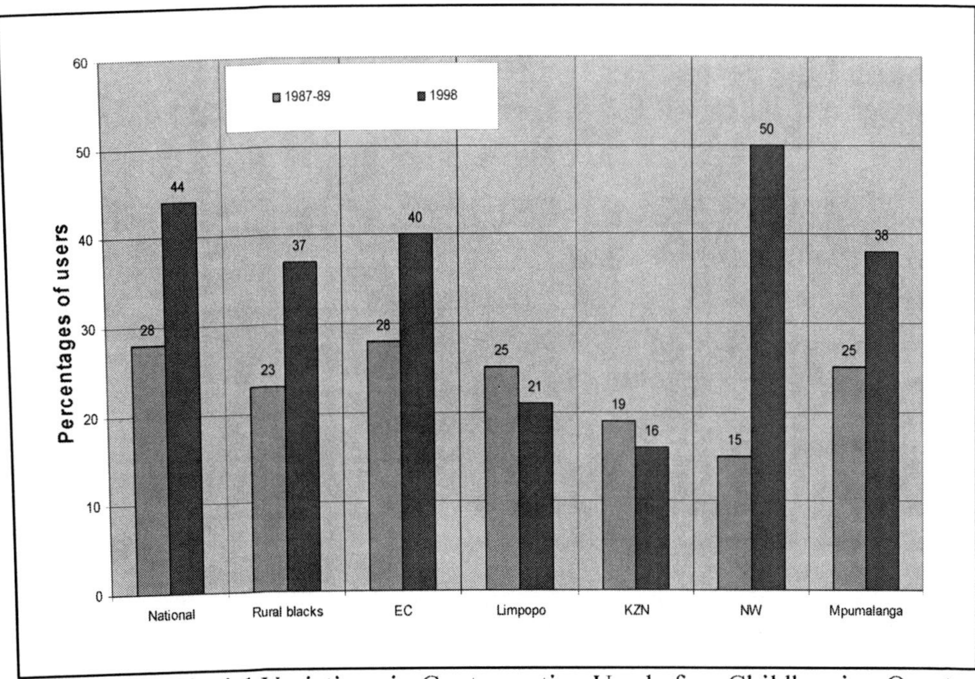

Figure 4.5 Provincial Variations in Contraceptive Use before Childbearing Onset, During 1987-9 and 1998

EC= Eastern Cape   KZN = KwaZulu-Natal   NW= North West

Contraception before onset of childbearing appeared to have a weak relationship with the age patterns of childbearing. For instance, KZN province rural women reflected lower use of contraception before onset of childbearing, along with a higher age at onset of childbearing compared to the other provinces. This suggests either higher levels of sexual abstinence or use of traditional methods of contraception to postpone childbearing onset. Conversely, the Mpumalanga and Eastern Cape reflected no demonstrable increase in ages at onset of childbearing in 1998, despite the increases in contraceptive use before childbearing onset.

4.2.4. *Contraceptive Method Use by Marital Status in the Selected Provinces*

Findings on analysis of methods used by married and single women nationally and in the various provinces in 1987–89 and 1998 Percentage of types of contraceptives are reflected on Figures 4.6 and 4.7, respectively. The 2004 data did not allow

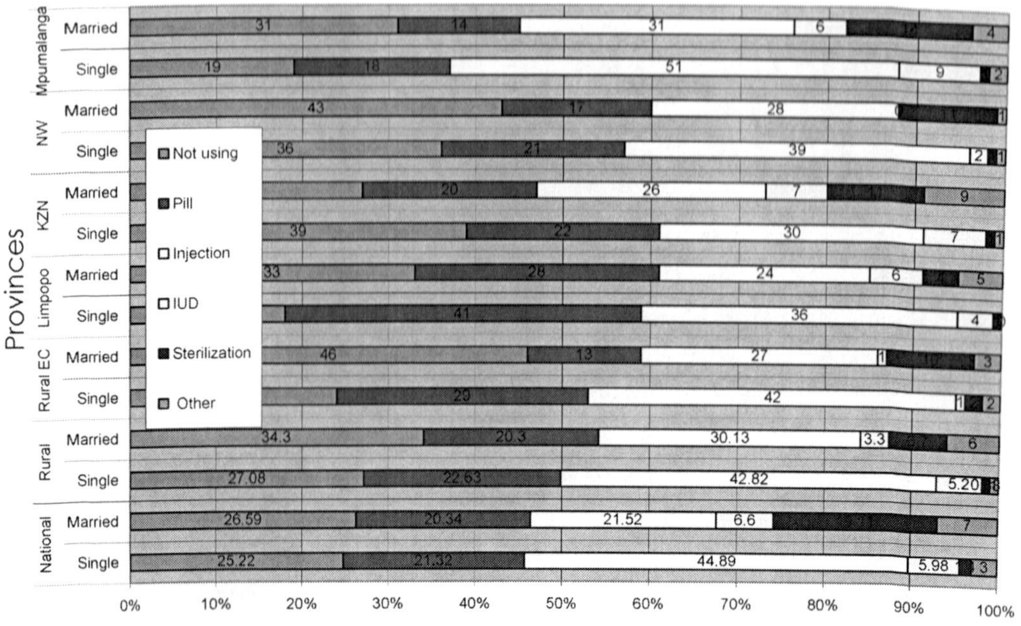

for analysis of this aspect.

Figure 4.6. Provincial Rural Contraceptive Method Use by Marital Status, 1987–89

Figure 4.6 reflects that in 1987–9, in each of the provincial contexts, larger percentages of married than unmarried women were not using contraception, except KwaZulu-Natal, where the percentage of non-use of contraception amongst single women exceeded non-use by married women. This, taken in conjunction with the higher age at onset of childbearing in KZN province that was noted in the previous sections of this work, suggests more reliance on sexual abstinence or use of traditional methods of contraception. The pill and the injection enjoyed the most usage amongst both married and single women in all the provinces, with the injection being marginally more utilized. IUD use reflected the lowest use percentages, while sterilization reflected substantially higher percentages of use amongst married than among single women.

The 1998 data reflected increases in non-use of contraception, both among married and unmarried women, as well as lower percentages in the use of both the pill and the IUD. Condom use reflected a marginal increase over the IUD. As is the case in 1987–9, the injection was the dominant method used by both married and unmarried women. The injection method was followed by the pill for single women, and by sterilization among married women. Sterilization among married women increased in all provinces except Mpumalanga, and its increase to 29 per cent in the Limpopo province exceeded the national figure of 17 per cent. The sterilization percentages amongst single women ranged from very low to negligible (Figure 4.7).

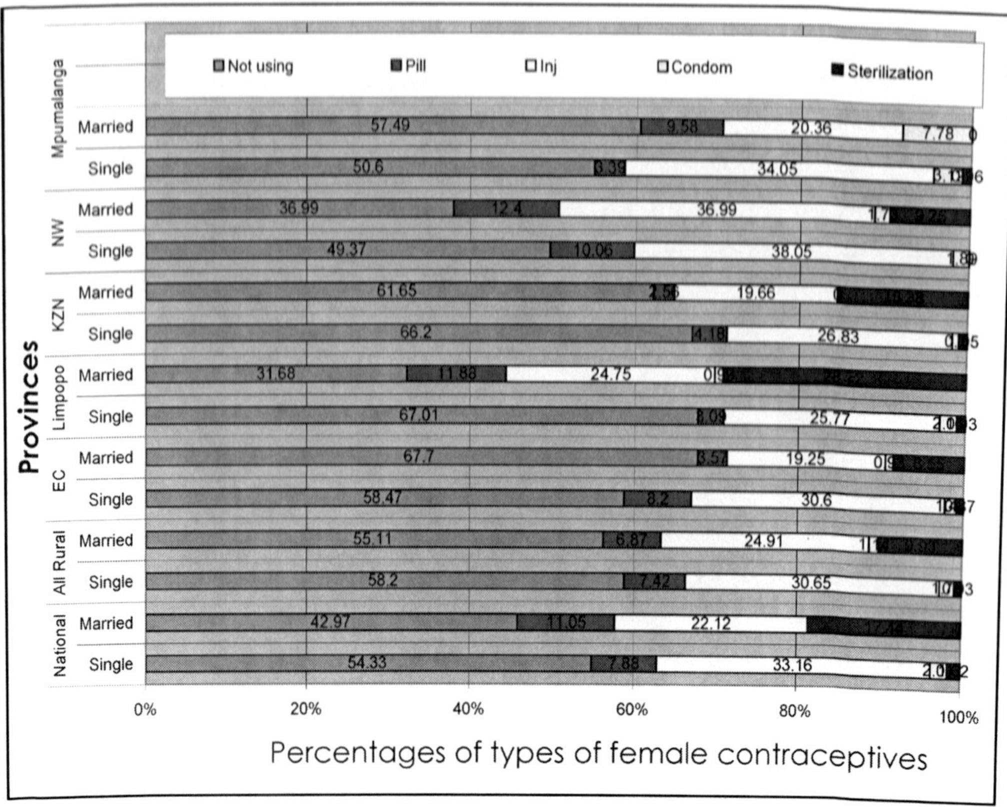

Figure 4.7 Rural Women's Contraceptive Method Choices by Martial Status, 1998

4.3 Findings on Analyses of Sterilizations

The samples for voluntary sterilizations were much smaller than those for childbirths and contraception, and the findings based on the various sub-samples must be treated with caution.

4.3.1 The Changes in Age Patterns of Rural Sterilizations

Analysis of the age patterns, in five year age cohorts, of women who requested for sterilizations   reflected that the modal age cohort for sterilizations shifted downwards from the 45–49 year age cohorts in 1987–9 to the 35–39 year age cohort in 1998, and finally to the 30–34 year age cohort in 2004, suggesting that more women request sterilization at younger ages than before (Table 4.6).

Table 4.6 Sterilization patterns of childbearing age women by age cohort

Age cohorts	Sterilization patterns (in percentages)		
	1987–89	1998	2004
<20	1	0	0
20–24	2	4	4
25–29	8	25	8
30–34	12	29	37
35–39	22	30	31
40–44	27	10	18
45–49	28	2	2
	100	100	100
Number	196	273	41

For analysis of sterilization requests by the parity of women requesting them, both the mean number of previous births to women requesting sterilization and groupings of women according to their previous childbirths were done.

4.3.2 *The Mean Previous Childbirths of Women Requesting Sterilization*

The mean number of previous childbirths at which women requested sterilizations increased between 1987–89 and 1998 both nationally and as the aggregate for rural women. Amongst the provinces, only the North West province reflected a drop in the mean number of children amongst women seeking sterilizations. For the rural Eastern Cape Province women, the mean increased further in 2004, reflecting a consistent upward trend; while the 2004 means for KwaZulu-Natal and the Mpumalanga Provinces decreased (Table 4.7). Analysis of requests for sterilizations using modal childbirths, however, reflected a different pattern.

Table 4.7 Mean number of previous births to women who requested sterilization

	Mean previous births to women (in number)		
	1987–89	1998	2004
All South Africa	3.05 (N=1518)	3.50 (N=1100)	na
Rural black women	4.10 (N=200)	4.30 (N=73)	4.30 (N=26)
Rural Eastern Cape	3.40 (N=61)	4.30 (N=71)	4.50 (N=9)
Rural Limpopo	3.30 (N=40)	3.50 (N=41)	na
Rural KwaZulu-Natal	4.00 (N=10)	4.40 (N=33)	4.00 (N=28)
Rural Mpumalanga	3.30 (N=29)	4.10 (N=31)	3.70 (N=17)
Rural North West	7.00 (N=10)	4.00 (N=26)	na

4.3.3 Percentage Distributions of Parities of Women Requesting Sterilizations in the Various Provinces in 1987–89

A more detailed and localized consideration of the parity of women who requested sterilizations in 1987–9 reflected that both nationally and for the rural Eastern Cape Province, three births was the modal parity at which women requested sterilization. The highest modal parity of five childbirths was reflected by the Limpopo, North-West and Mpumalanga provinces and was also the modal parity for rural women (Figure 4.8).

KZN Province women had a modal parity of four childbirths, and Eastern Cape Province women had a modal parity of a little more than three childbirths, which was equivalent to the national mode. Regarding the provincial variations of parities at which women requested sterilizations, the modal parity of four childbirths for KZN represented 40 per cent of sterilizations cases, and an additional 30 per cent of women requested sterilizations after their second births, the highest figure for sterilizations at second births nationally (Figure 4.8).

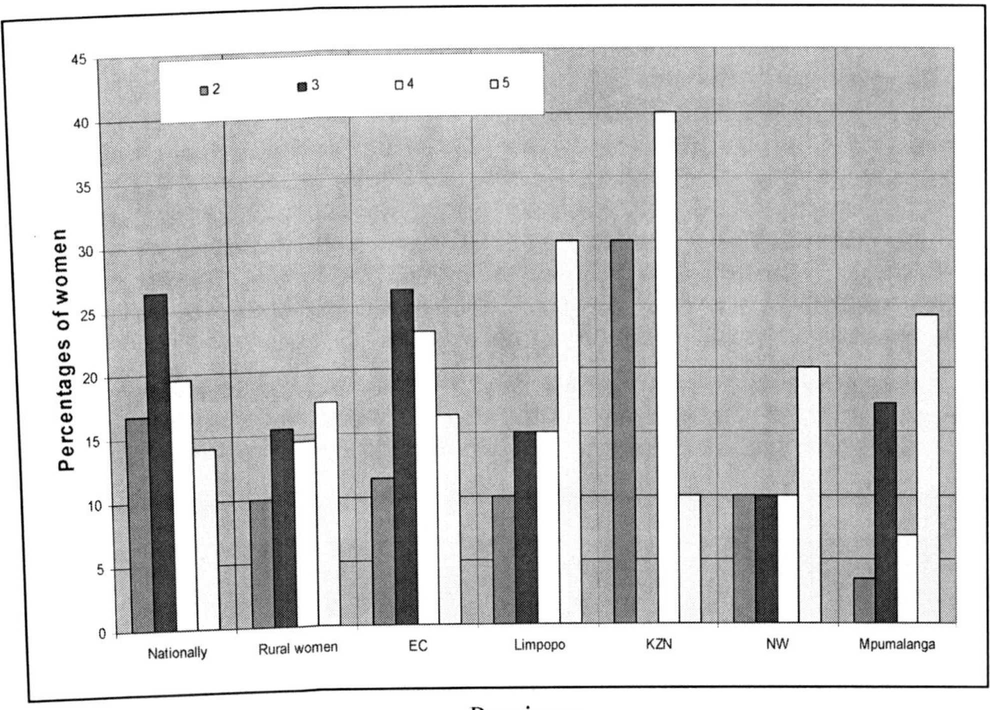

Figure 4.8 Parties at which Rural Women Requested Sterilzations, 1987–89

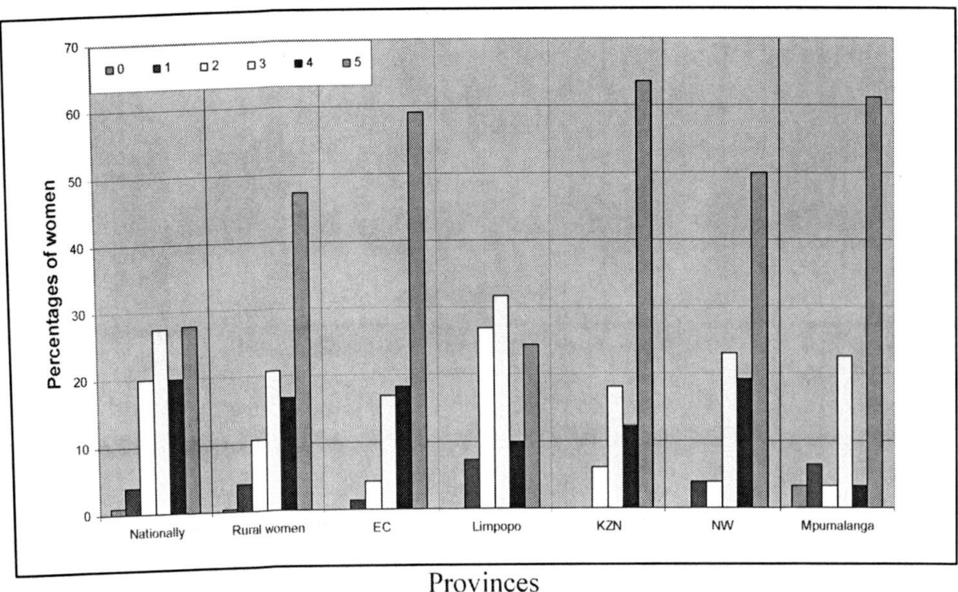

Figure 4.9. Parities at which Women in Various Provinces Requested Sterilization, 1998

The 1998 data on sterilization requests reflected that the EC, KZN the NW and Mpumalanga provinces all had modal parities of five childbirths for women requesting sterilizations, and this was the modal parity for all rural women requesting sterilizations. These modal percentages were all higher than 40 per cent of all sterilizations, and for Mpumalanga and KZN were above 60 per cent of the total requests for sterilizations. Only the Limpopo province women had a modal parity of three childbirths at requesting sterilization. The Limpopo province also had the highest percentage of women requesting sterilizations after their second childbirths across the provinces compared and nationally (Figure 4.9).

The three provinces for which data for 2004 was available reflect a wide range of parities at which women request sterilization, ranging from two to nine childbirths. The modal parity was two childbirths (Figure 4.10).

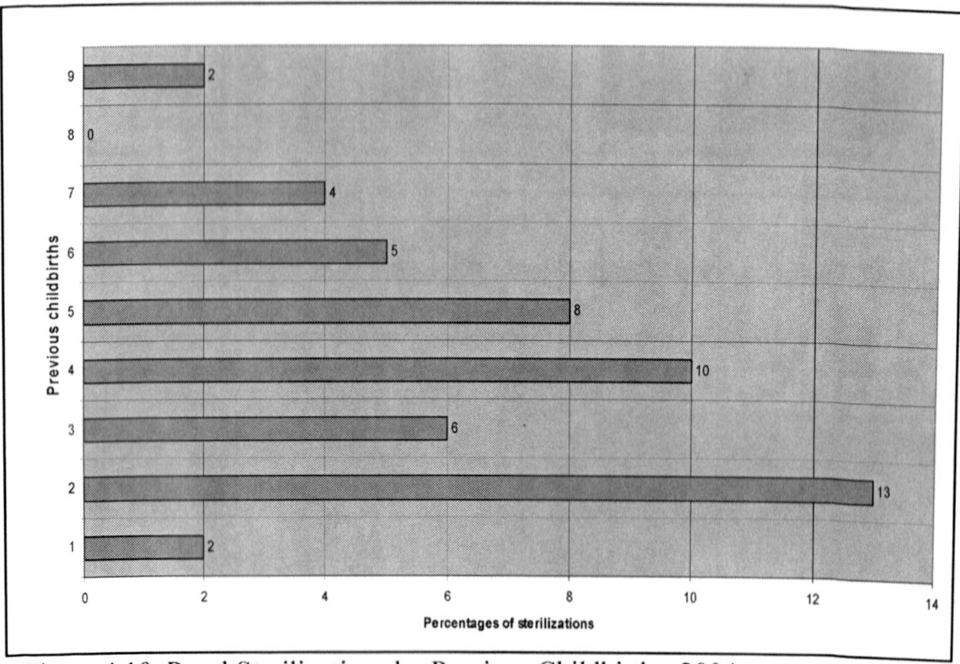

Figure 4.10. Rural Sterilizations by Previous Childbirths, 2004

4.3.4 Provincial Variations in Rural Sterilizations by Women's Marital Status

Although sterilizations amongst single women increased between 1987–9 and 1998, they remained below the threshold of 20 per cent of total sterilizations for each province, and married women generally accounted for more than 80 per cent of the sterilizations that were done in their respective provinces. In the KwaZulu-Natal Province, all sterilization clients were married women in 1987–89, while in 1998, this was the case in the North-West and Limpopo provinces. While the use of sterilization amongst single women reflected a decline from the 1987–89 level in 1998 nationally, it reflected a modest increase amongst rural women. This increase was fairly large in the Eastern Cape, KwaZulu-Natal and Mpumalanga Provinces (Figure 4.11).

Figure 4.11 Rural Sterilizations by Women's Marital Status in the Various Provinces, during 1987–89 and 1998

As presented in Figure 4.11, nationally, among married women, the percentage of sterilizations increased from the 1987–9 levels in 1998, but among rural women, there was a fall in this percentage. This decline appears to be accounted for by the trends in the Eastern Cape, KwaZulu-Natal and Mpumalanga Provinces. Married women in the Limpopo and North-West Provinces reflected increases in percentages of sterilizations during the same period.

The overall age and parity scenario for rural women's requests for sterilizations suggested a decline in the age trend for requests, but the trend in the parities at which women requested sterilizations reflected a clear directional consistency. Although sterilizations are predominantly used by married women, growing percentages of single women are using them too.

4.4 Findings on Patterns of Pregnancy Terminations

Also data on pregnancy termination requests was small, and the findings reported on were based on all the cases that actually had pregnancy terminations, since some requests were turned down for various reasons. Data for 1998 was historical: it was based on women's responses on whether they ever had a pregnancy termination during the course of their reproductive lives, and many of the terminations referred to occurred before pregnancy termination was legalized in November 1996.

4.4.1 The Historical Age Patterns of Pregnancy Terminations

During the 1998 SADHS, 11.2 per cent of the sample of the 11,735 childbearing age women interviewed nationally responded that they had used pregnancy termination previously. The percentage was 11.3 amongst black rural women, from a sample of 5,217 cases.

The age composition of this pregnancy termination sample by provinces amongst rural black women   reflected the ages at which pregnancy terminations actually occurred. The age pattern of pregnancy terminations suggested that nationally, pregnancy terminations occurred largely amongst the 20–24 and 25–29 year age cohorts, except in the North-West Province, in which the 30–34 year age cohort had the largest percentage of pregnancy terminations (Figure 4.12). The Limpopo province had the fewest incidences of termination of pregnancy (TOPs), and these were evenly spread across the 30–34 and 40–44 age cohorts. Except for these two provincial exceptions, the three other provinces largely fell in with the national pattern and shaped the overall age pattern for rural women's pregnancy terminations accordingly. The 40–49 age cohorts was either minimally represented or not represented in some provinces.

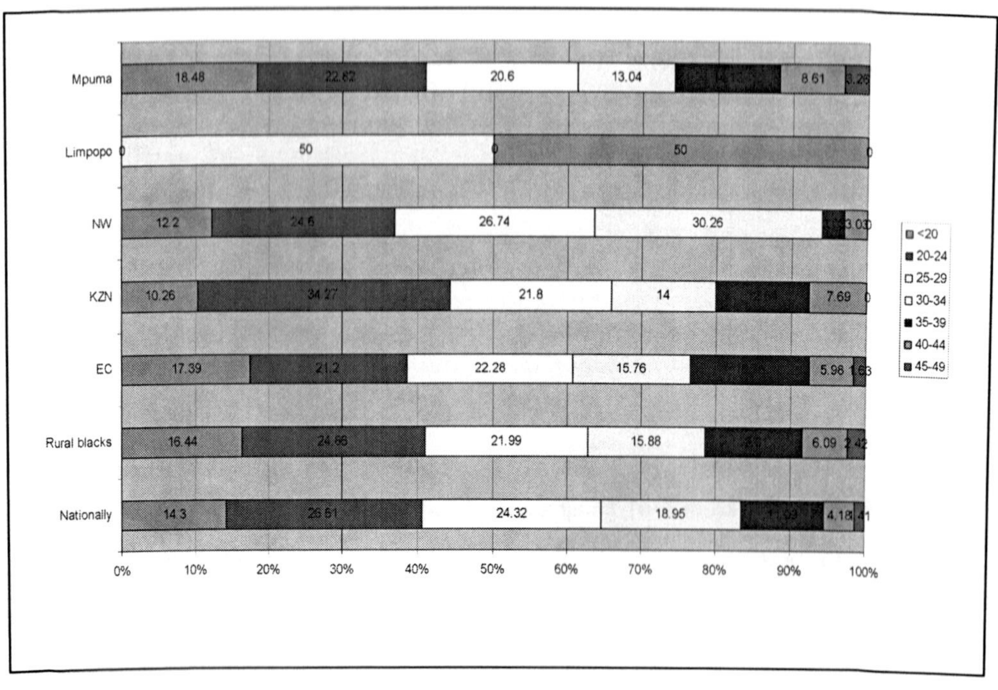

Figure 4.12. The Historical Age Patterns of TOPs by Rural Women.

The age pattern of pregnancy terminations that took place after the
:ption of 1996 Choice of Termination of Pregnancy Act is reflected in
ire 4.13 in a comparison of the national and black rural women's trends.
comparison revealed that rural women had a slightly higher percentage
regnancy terminations than the national population amongst the under-
ige cohort, as well as for the 40–44 and 45–49 age cohorts. For the age
....orts between these two extremes, rural pregnancy terminations either
equalled the national percentages or fell below it. The comparison

suggested that the demand for pregnancy terminations amongst rural women was spread across all ages.

The comparison of the age patterns of rural pregnancy termination for 1998 and 2004 indicated a higher incidence of pregnancy terminations among the three youngest age cohorts of rural women in 2004, compared to the 1998 pattern, but after the 25–29 age cohort, the 2004 rural pregnancy terminations progressively dropped below the 1998 trend line, ending with the 40–44 age cohort.

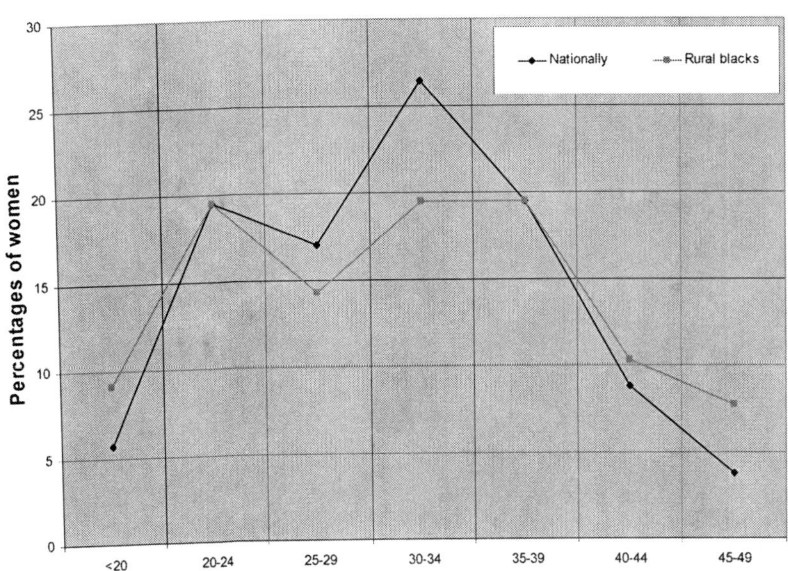

Figure 4.13. National and Rural Age Patterns of Pregnancy Terminations, 1997–98

4.4.2 Previous Childbirth History of Women Requesting Pregnancy Terminations

Nationally and in the Eastern Cape Province, birth orders of five and above had the highest TOP requests in 1998. For the aggregate of rural women, this category of high order births had the second largest percentage of TOPs. The Limpopo Province was the only province that had its highest percentage of requests after the first childbirths. Overall, requests for pregnancy terminations largely followed the second and third order births, and women with zero childbirths had the lowest percentages of TOPs in all the categories compared (Figure 4.14).

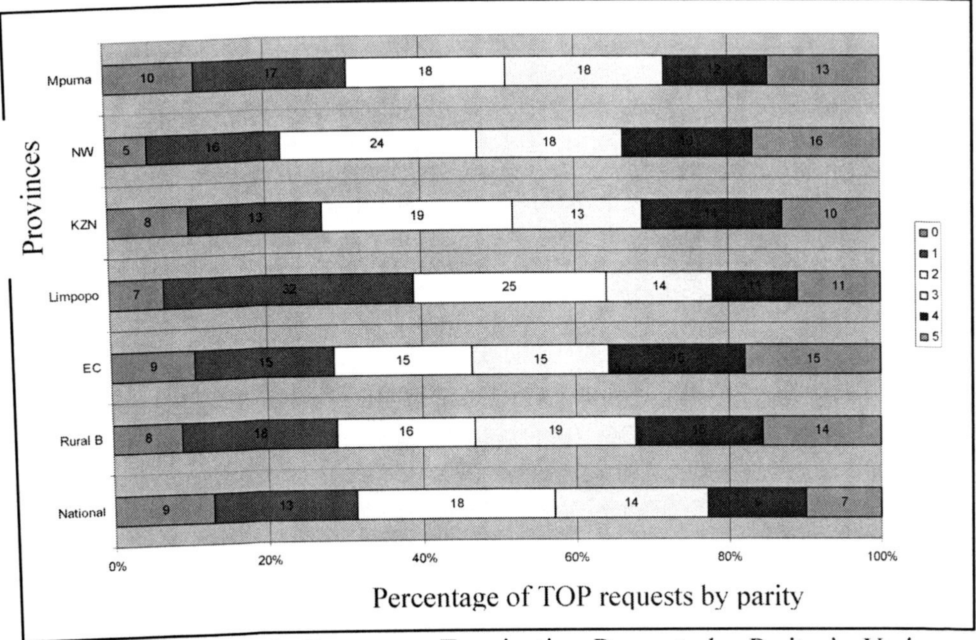

Figure 4.14 Women's Pregnancy Termination Requests by Parity in Various Provinces

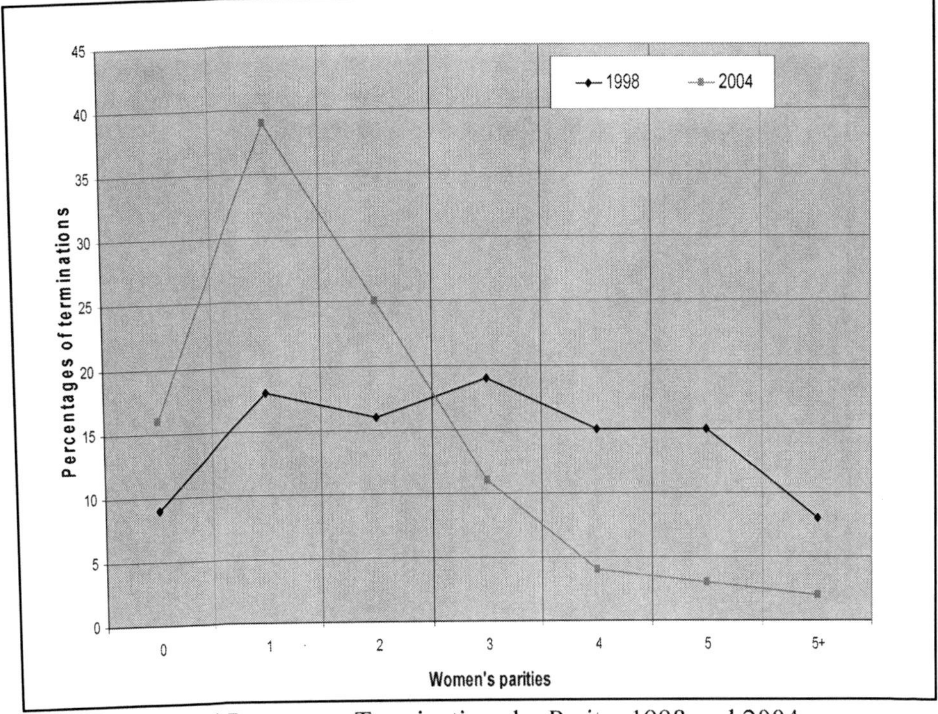

Figure 4.15 Rural Pregnancy Terminations by Parity, 1998 and 2004

From a comparison of the 1998 and 2004 data on rural pregnancy terminations by previous childbirths (Figure 4.15), there was an increase in 2004 than in 1998 in percentage of rural women who terminate pregnancies at zero childbirths, thus postponing childbearing. However, the largest increase in pregnancy terminations followed the first childbirth. After the second childbirth, pregnancy terminations were still much higher amongst rural women in 2004 than in 1998. After the third and subsequent childbirths, TOPs in 2004 remained much lower than TOP in the 1998 rural samples, indicating pregnancy terminations as having relevance predominantly in regulating childbirths at lower parities (Figure 4.15).

4.5 A Summary of the Salient Findings from Data Analysis

The findings reported on in this chapter indicated an upward trend in the age pattern of onset and progression of childbearing amongst rural women, as well as a fall in the mean number of children born per woman. However, trends among married and single women were contrasting, with the single women's predominance determining the overall directional trend, except in sterilization trends, which are dominated by married women. Both contraception and pregnancy terminations are dominated by the 20–24 and 25 to 29 year age cohorts. Rural women progressively request sterilizations at younger ages but at higher parities. The overall findings indicated accessibility of a wide range reproductive health services to rural women, although provincial and sub-provincial variations could not be established from this analysis. The rural Eastern Cape Province appeared to be lagging behind the other provinces in several of the changes that are taking place amongst the provincial rural populations compared.

CHAPTER 5
DISCUSSION OF THE FINDINGS

It is worth noting at the outset of this discussion, as the 1994 Programme of Action recommends, that the enormous role men can play in the changes set out herein cannot be sufficiently highlighted. Added to that, strategies for taking men on board to the changes that are taking place as reproductive partners are not just warranted but are mandatory. The rural character of the subject population recalls the discovery made on regulation of childbirths amongst working class women in western societies at the end of the 18th century, which prompted the observation that "… the art of fooling nature was not the exclusive privilege of city dwellers and libertines but was known and practiced by those who, being close to nature itself, should have held it to be more repugnant than anyone else did" (Foucault 1978, 121).

Even though the reproductive aspirations of black rural women in South Africa have changed in recent years, they lag behind those of their urban counterparts (South African Demographic and Health Survey 1998). That is the case despite the powerful agency of rural-urban interactions in the country. Both cultural factors and inadequate accessibility of reproductive health services to some rural populations might be the underlying factors in the differential pace of reproductive behaviour patterns observed between rural and urban women.

The findings of this analysis provide an evaluation of achievements on reproductive changes amongst rural women on the basis of the recommendations made in the 1994 Programme of Action, which provides the guiding principles for South Africa's reproductive health service provision agenda. Secondly, the research findings were evaluated against rural women's views on their reproductive aspirations as revealed by the focus group discussions (Mfono 2002). Thirdly, the findings were evaluated on their demographic transition implications. Fourthly, the phenomenon of non-marital childbearing that is pervasive in the subject population was also evaluated for its economic, demographic and wider social implications, and in comparison with similar situations elsewhere. Next, the AIDS epidemic underlying the reproductive behaviour scenario is was considered. Finally, the discussion considered the policy and research implications that emanate from the research findings.

5.1 The Emerging Reproductive Behavioural Patterns Viewed against the 1994 Programme of Action

The findings of a median age of 20 years at onset of childbearing suggest that approximately half of first rural childbirths in the research context occur to women who are about 20 years old, with the majority of them in their late adolescence. This threshold, while above the upper limit of the compulsory school-age of 16 years encroaches on secondary school enrolment, posing a challenge to the educational advancement of girls. Accessibility of contraception to sexually active adolescents who might want to postpone the onset of childbearing until they have completed high school education thus remains critical. Whilst the childcare grants provided by the government since 1994 obviously benefit these young mothers, childbirths that detract young women from formal schooling constitute a problem from women's social developmental perspective. Such childbearing also imposes economic pressure on the parents of adolescents, making investment on further education of the affected adolescents difficult.

Adolescent vulnerability to sexual coercion is so widespread amid the pervasive sexual violence in South Africa that some adolescents who are not sexually active reported at the focus group discussions that they use contraception to protect themselves from conception, in the event of such coercion (Mfono 2002). From the focus group discussions, it also emerged that amongst adolescents, 18 years was considered an acceptable age of child-bearing onset, if the woman has an income source for supporting the child. This normative age for childbearing onset amongst adolescents could be of critical significance, because of the strong peer pressure which prevails within this age group. However, another perspective generated from focus group discussions with children of 6–12 years and adolescents of 13–18 years by Bility (1996, 6) is that pregnancy for some adolescents is a means to an end; it allows them to leave home and quit a school situation which they consider as alienating. Childbearing thus accelerates their entry into adulthood and independence from parents, especially where sexual relationships have material incentives.

The complexity of the adolescent scenario was elaborated on in the 1994 Programme of Action's observation that in many societies, adolescents face pressure to engage in sexual activity, that adolescents from low income backgrounds are highly vulnerable with limited life choices which nullify incentives to avoid pregnancy and childbearing. The question of rural adolescents' alternative life opportunities to mothering in South Africa is both politically and socially challenging, within the rural poverty context.

In the study conducted in the rural Victoria East District, Mfono (2002) found from focus group discussions that traditional parental resistance to adolescent contraception has been replaced by parental encouragement because of the concerns about the economic pressure that early childbearing imposes on limited household resources. Participants of the adolescent focus group discussions also noted that the economic needs of the affected adolescent mother shift to a secondary priority in parental budgets when there is a baby in the household. Thus adolescents' recognition of babies as favoured competitors for limited family resources might provide them with an incentive for postponing childbirth.

The increase in adolescent childbirths in 1998 and 2004 compared to 1987–89 might be an outcome of a preponderance of single women in the samples during the latter years, with their lower mean ages at childbearing onset. Provincial median ages at childbearing onset ranged from 18 years in Mpumalanga to 21 years in KwaZulu Natal in 1987–89. Such variations were apparently not the outcome of contraceptive use patterns before childbearing onset, which were low in KwaZulu Natal and the Limpopo Provinces in 1998, compared to the other provinces. The differences might be attributable to differential adolescent exposure to conception in the different provinces. The provincial convergence of median ages at onset of childbearing in 1998 could similarly be indicative of more uniform marital patterns, with unmarried women pulling down the mean ages at childbearing onset because of their predominance in the samples. The 2004 provincial ages at onset of childbearing reflected a range of four years, from 19–22 years, with Mpumalanga Province reflecting a consistent upward trend, while the Eastern Cape Province reflected consistently downward mean ages.

The consistent decline in the proportions of married women in the samples of childbearing women obscures their contribution to the mean ages of childbearing onset, which in 1998 and 2004 was higher than those for single women. The overall age at onset of childbearing is thus the outcome of contrasting directional trends in ages at childbearing onset between married and single women.

The scenario of wider mean spacing of lower order births observed from the research findings causes a shifting of childbearing to older ages. This trend could be associated with longer periods taken by reproductive couples to consolidate economic stability that allows them to have additional children. Childbearing decisions subsequent to the first birth appeared to be contingent on the unfolding of economic circumstances, rather than being piecemeal. As elucidated by participants of the focus group discussions, even though child spacing in its own right has health and social significance for women, there are overriding economic considerations in decisions about each subsequent birth. Overall, childbearing progression was also attended by a fairly high incidence of both contraceptive use as well as pregnancy terminations, and ultimately of sterilizations.

The findings on the age pattern of progression to higher order births reflected much more dynamism between 1998 and 2004, compared to the earlier research period. The spacing of childbirths amongst rural women appeared to be widening, with the old African tradition on child spacing being endorsed by the health and demographic outlooks on childbearing. In the study conducted among rural women in the Victoria East district, Mfono (2002) found that all the age cohort focus group participants endorsed wide spacing of children and placed the onus for such spacing on the woman. Closely-spaced children were referred to as "steps", a label which summoned suppressed smiles that indicated the shamefulness of a woman allowing that eventuality to find its way into her child-bearing progression. Various years between births were suggested, but consensus amongst the participants was that the wider the spacing between births, the better the outcome.

The findings of this research also reflected that very wide spacing of lower order births is followed by progressively narrower spacing of higher order births. Various factors might explain this trend. In the South African context, the first childbirth frequently comes before marriage. If the woman subsequently gets married to a man who is not the father of the first child, she most likely faces a new childbearing agenda, which, being informed by the dictates of the lobola (bride-wealth) custom, may include a requirement of male offspring and a minimum number of surviving offspring. When women marry late, they might want to "catch up" on the desired number and sex of children, in the face of advancing age. This argument commands a high probability in the face of the high marital age amongst black women, which ranges between 29 years (Udjo 1996) and 30 years (Budlender, Chobokoane, and Simelane 2004).

The spacing of second births was noted as having the largest mean number of years, suggesting that after the onset of childbearing, the occurrence of the second birth is consciously delayed for an extended period by many women. This was also reflected in the increase in use of contraception and pregnancy terminations after the first childbirth. This could suggest that the first childbirth is followed by hardships which cause many women to want to postpone childbearing for as long as possible. As first childbirths largely occur amongst unmarried women, within the poverty context in which many rural households live, first childbirths most likely bring hardship to the families of their mothers, despite the child care grants provided by the government.

It has also been argued that South Africa's practice of allowing teenage mothers to return to school once they have given birth produces a long delay before the birth of a second child (Kaufman, de Wet and Stadler 2000). Mfono (2002) also found from focus group discussions that after the first premarital childbirth, women face strong pressure, both from their peers and from wider society, against having a second birth before marriage or economic independence. The flippant outlook of fathers to their offspring and their mothers most likely provides a wake-up call to many young mothers, who, after their first childbirth, find themselves on their own, against economic and other outcomes of unprotected sexual involvement. These hardships probably warn them to avoid or delay similar occurrences until they are ready for the challenges that might come with them. More importantly, the prevalent postponement of second childbirths amongst rural women also indicates their achievement of control over their reproduction. The first childbirth appears to release the capabilities of both service providers and service users to work in unison towards delaying the occurrence of an unplanned second birth, a scenario that appears to be much weaker before the first childbirth.

Child spacing appeared to be emerging as a more strongly defining feature of the populations considered in this research than is postponement of childbearing onset. This demonstrates rural women's dominant orientation in the use of reproductive health technology in accordance with realities confronting them.

According to the various national surveys, South African rural women's childbearing aspirations are changing in a downward direction. In agreement with the national surveys reviewed, this analysis also reflected that growing proportions of women of childbearing age had zero childbirth during the 1998 and 2004 periods, compared to the 1987–9 period. Although this may partly be the outcome of different sampling approaches, growing school attendance, especially compulsory school attendance after 1994 may also be changing the priorities of parents and young girls. Women with one birth consistently formed the largest proportion of childbearing women over the periods considered. The proportion of this group reflected a modest increase from its 1998 level in 2004, which might be associated with the growth in the representation of single women in childbearing, with their predominant contribution to lower order births. Subsequent birth orders reflected progressive declines during the periods compared, with steeper declines between 1998 and 2004 reflecting the pace of decline in proportions of higher order births in recent years. These changes affected the mean number of children ever born to women of childbearing age in the populations considered, which reflected a progressive decline over the periods considered in this research.

The analysis of the scenario of lowering birth rates amongst women in Southern Africa, despite the levels of poverty led Potts and Marks (2001) to the conclusion that adverse economic conditions in this context create a demand for fertility regulation. They note that the Southern African scenario challenges the traditional theoretical outlook that improved economic conditions are a prerequisite for a decline in birth rates, observing that demographic surveys in poor countries reveal that women want fewer children because they cannot afford more. This suggests that women are forgoing some children in order to sustain consumption for themselves and their existing children at current levels. They choose new improved and higher consumption, instead of children, as argued by the traditional economic views on fertility regulation. Potts and Marks, however, also express the view that the relatively better socio-economic conditions in Southern Africa, compared to what the situation is in many sub-Saharan African countries, are behind the positive response of African women in the region to fertility regulation measures.

Where provincial variations in mean number of children ever born are concerned, all the provinces reflected means of less than three children during the three time periods compared. The Eastern Cape Province reflected the highest mean in 1987–9, with a decline during the two subsequent periods, even though a consistent directional trend has yet to emerge. This scenario must be understood against the fact that the Eastern Cape Province is the second poorest province in South Africa, and the possibility of interplay between poverty and women's childbearing patterns. The mean CEB for rural KwaZulu-Natal province increased during the period between 1987–9 and 1998 but dropped dramatically thereafter. KwaZulu-Natal is known to be the severest affected province by the AIDS epidemic, a reality that might lie behind the dramatic drop in the 2004 mean CEB. The North-West, Limpopo, and Mpumalanga provinces also reflected declines in mean number of children ever born between the two national surveys. The 2004 mean CEB trend for Mpumalanga also reflected this consistent downward trend, while 2004 data was not available for the North-West and Limpopo provinces.

The rural provincial directional trends in mean CEB are consistent with the 1998 SADHS women's expressed views on desired number of children. The scenario also suggests that women have reasonable access to reproductive health services that enable them to meet their expressed reproductive health needs. However, the various rural contexts also have diverse scenarios of poverty, educational achievement amongst women and access and use of reproductive health services.

Realizing how some rural populations tend to remain at the margins with regard to service access, Hutchison, Boerma, and Khan (2004) classified the population of the Eastern Cape Province into sub-regional municipal district populations as rural former Transkei and the rural and urban non-Transkei and commercial farming district populations. They noted the gap between the former Transkei and the other rural areas in the various demographic changes. The differential achievements between the various Eastern Cape geographic municipal districts (see Map of Eastern Cape Province) are presented in Table 5.1. The analysis points to the need to go beyond the provincial to district analyses, to identify the achievements and lags in addressing rural women's reproductive health needs.

Table 5.1. Rural settlement, reproductive and IMR in Eastern Cape Province regions

District Municipality	Predominant settlement	No. of clinics	Mean distance to clinic (km)	IMR**	TFR***	Women on contraception (%)
OR Tambo	Former Transkei	157	6.6	94/1000	5	38
Alfred Nzo	Former Transkei	28	7.7	88/1000	4.1	24
Chris Hani	Former Transkei	116	4.0	57/1000	3.1	61
Amatole	Rural Non-Transkei and Urban	189	3.6	34/1000	2.8	70
Ukhwahlamba	Former Transkei & CFD*	25	2.7	53/1000	3.2	71
Western	CFD	53	11.9	54/1000	2.1	84
Nelson Mandela	Urban Non-Transkei	55	2.0	38/1000	2.4	68

SOURCE: Adapted from Hutchinson, Boerma, and Khan (2004)

*Commercial Farming Districts   **IMR= infant mortality rate   ***TMR= total mortality rate

Data in Table 5.1 indicates that the three former Transkei municipal districts emerge as lagging behind the other district municipalities in infant mortality, total fertility rates and percentages of women on contraception. These three municipal districts have the largest rural populations in the Eastern Cape Province, and that pulls down the demographic and health indicators reflected by the rural Eastern Cape Province populations. Even though the Ukhwahlamba and Western District Municipalities also have predominantly rural populations, they appear to have much better reproductive health than the three former Transkei regions have. It appears from Table 5.1 that higher contraceptive use amongst women in these districts is matched by declines in infant mortality.

In sub-provincial analyses of the South African Human Development Index (HDI) Whiteford, Posel, and Kelatwang (1995) found that the rural black populations living in the former Ciskei districts (now constituting the Amatole District Municipality) had HDIs that were much higher than for those living in the rest of the rural Eastern Cape Province, with only a narrow gap between them and those of blacks living in the Eastern Cape urban areas. It is therefore not surprising to find similarities between their indicators on reproductive health service access and infant mortality and those of the predominantly urban Nelson Mandela Municipal District. The significant point that emerges from these dynamics on the reproductive scenario of the rural Eastern Cape Province women is that of varying conditions of accessibility of services within the province, with district lags that warrant attention. Such sub-provincial differentials may well apply in the other provinces between rural populations living in different sub-regions.

The difference between married and single women in the mean CEB warrants discussion within the South African context, in which the incidence of non-marital childbearing is high. While rural married women reflected a mean CEB that approximated three children, the mean CEB amongst single women was closer to one child. This difference of approximately two children between the two groups is probably attributable to differential exposures of the two groups of women to conception. To some extent, married women are probably also confronted by the cultural demand for male offspring, as well as by defined normative childbirth numbers. This difference is indicative of the reproductive regulatory capabilities of rural women which are enhanced by reproductive health services. In the context of the opposing reproductive directional changes amongst rural women, unmarried women, through their numerical predominance, exert a downward pull on the overall mean CEB, thus contributing to lowering the birth rates of rural women. Analysis of the 1996 South African census data revealed that the total marital fertility for black women nationally was 27 per cent higher than the total fertility rate for all black women (Udjo 1996). This was attributed to the sum effects of non-marriage, age at marriage and intervals between marriages.

The patterns of contraceptive use that bring about these scenarios are now considered, beginning with adolescent contraception. In addition to constituting the largest reproductive age cohorts amongst women in developing countries, adolescents are a special category of reproductive age women. Their vulnerability and needs differ from those of older reproductive age cohorts of women. Service providers might also dismiss their claims to reproductive health services as illegitimate, while some adolescents may consider their sexual involvement as an embarrassment that must be a guarded secret to professional health workers as adults. But the 1994 Programme of Action assigned the responsibility of providing adolescents with appropriate direction and guidance in sexual and reproductive matters to both parents and other persons responsible for adolescents. It also recommended accessibility of appropriate reproductive health services and information necessary to adolescents, including information on sexually transmitted diseases and sexual abuse. The rights of adolescents to privacy, confidentiality, informed consent, respect of cultural values and religious beliefs were also highlighted in the United Nations' recommendations on removal of legal, regulatory and social barriers to reproductive health information and care to adolescents.

Since the inception of South Africa's democratic dispensation, the South African government has used the recommendations contained in the 1994 Programme of Action as the guideline for the principles of reproductive service provision. Mfono's analysis of rural women's reproductive behavioural trends in the Victoria East District of the Eastern Cape Province (Mfono 2002) also revealed that contraceptive service use was dominated by adolescents, who also constituted the largest of reproductive age cohorts in that population. However, this may have been the trend in that specific rural population, a trend that probably emulates the trend amongst urban adolescents. As indicated in Table 4.5, contraceptive use amongst rural women in the subject populations was dominated by the 20–24 year age cohorts during the periods considered in this research, and not by adolescents, who constitute the largest reproductive age cohort. Adolescents assumed the third position as current contraceptive users in 1987–9 and 1998, and dropped to the fourth position in 2004. This may be a product of various factors. Social factors like attitudes on childbearing onset as well as accessibility and perceived legitimacy of contraception might be the underlying factors. In addition, as the Plan of Action points out, adolescents with no other perceived life opportunities might not see the point of postponing childbearing.

Garenne, Tollman, and Kahn (2000) attribute the observed high incidence of pre-marital fertility in South Africa to a low incidence of both contraceptive and abortion use before the first birth amongst adolescents. Family planning is thus viewed as failing to address the contraceptive needs of young women before their first pregnancy, and postponement of childbearing onset may be an insurmountable challenge in South African rural women's reproductive context. Also Cleland and Ali (2004) identified non-use of contraception as the dominant direct cause of unintended births.

Contraceptive use amongst the older reproductive age cohorts provides testimony on the accessibility of services to rural women, as well as lower perceived social and other barriers to their use. The occupational categories of current contraceptive users is constituted by scholars, housewives, women in a small variety of skilled and unskilled occupations, and a significantly large proportion of unemployed women, mostly in the 20–24 and 25–29 year age cohorts. The effectiveness of such use was observable in the spacing of childbirths, particularly the delay in second childbirths, which reflected prominence in the 2004 data. High rural unemployment along with low participation in tertiary education probably leaves many rural women stranded about life paths to follow, with the decline in marital incidence, and after the first childbirth, childbearing appears to lose attractiveness as well. The 30–34 years age cohort also reflected growing contraceptive use over the periods compared, but less strongly. Contraceptive use by older age cohorts reflected a declining trend over the periods considered. These overall trends appear to suggest adequate contraceptive accessibility, around which age norms for use are emerging amongst rural women.

The 1987–9 contraceptive method choices reflected both similarities and differences amongst married and single women. Non-use of contraception was higher amongst married than amongst single women. The use of reversible methods was similar amongst the two groups; the predominant reversible methods used being the injection and the pill. IUD use was low and sterilization use even lower. Sterilization was, however, more popular amongst married than amongst single women, but was much lower than the national percentage which was close to 20 per cent of all women currently using contraception. For all rural married women it was seven per cent, but four provinces had 10 per cent and above, and only the Limpopo Province reflected a low sterilization of four per cent. Accessibility of sterilization services to the various rural provincial populations may be the determinant of the differential use of this method by married women, amongst whom the demand for this service is apparently high.

Contraceptive method changes in 1998 were characterized by increases in the use of injection in all provinces, both amongst married and single women, as well as a marginal increase in sterilization amongst single women. A dramatic increase in sterilizations amongst married women in the Limpopo Province to 29 per cent was also noted, which exceeded the national level of 17 per cent. In other provinces, sterilizations amongst married women increased from the 1987–9 level, except in Mpumalanga Province, where it decreased. Once more, these trends can be viewed as reflecting both rural women's preference and accessibility of the methods used.

Over the research period, the age at which rural women requested sterilization reflected a downward shift from being dominated by the 40–44 and 45–49 year age cohorts in 1987–89 to a dominance of the 30–34 and 35-39 years age cohorts during the two subsequent time periods. However, the 40–44 years age cohort still reflected a strong presence in 2004, although the sample used was much smaller than the samples for the two earlier time periods. This downward shift in the ages at which women request sterilization might be viewed as indicative of an emerging desire to put an earlier age limit to childbearing for various reasons, including a stronger confidence in the survival of the children women already have.

The mean parity at which rural women requested voluntary sterilization, however, reflected an upward trend, ranging from 4.1 children in 1987-89 to 4.3 in 1998 and 2004. The provincial variations in mean previous childbirths were wide in 1987–89, ranging from seven in the North West Province to 3.3 in the Limpopo and Mpumalanga provinces, and probably reflected accessibility of the service to rural women. For 1998 and 2004, the provincial variations were much smaller, suggesting more equitable accessibility across provinces. The modal parities at which women requested sterilizations, however, varied across provinces. The highest modal parity of 5 or more childbirths in 1987–9 was reflected by women in the Limpopo Province, but this parity had plummeted to two childbirths in 1998. For the other four provinces, the 1987–9 modal parity for requesting sterilizations was three children, but shifted upwards to five children in 1998. This upward shift in the modal parity for sterilization requests between 1987–9 and 1998 might be attributable to the earlier intensity of the marketing of sterilizations, which emanated from the demographic rationale for regulation of births. By 1998, that pressure on women had dissipated, and the modal parities for requesting sterilizations probably reflected women's considered choices and less persuasion. The 2004 modal parity for rural sterilization requests was two children, but the sample was too small for provincial trend analysis.

Sterilizations amongst married rural women can also be viewed as reflecting a softening of male attitudes to childbearing limitation. Because of the irreversibility of its outcome, decision-making on sterilization has to be made by couples jointly. Through negotiation and skilful bargaining, married women are thus playing a critical role in extending the acceptance of women's reproductive aspirations to husbands, and possibly to their in-law families. Their agency role in the reproductive changes that are taking place challenges reproductive traditions.

Pregnancy terminations present monumental challenges to the emerging rural reproductive scenario. The 1998 survey's historical data on pregnancy terminations revealed that women had used pregnancy terminations at different ages during their reproductive years, even before it was legalized in South Africa. As with contraception, the 20–24 years and 25–29 years age cohorts had dominated the use of pregnancy terminations. During the

1997–8 period, black rural women also had higher proportions of TOPs amongst adolescents, compared to women nationally. The proportion of TOPs amongst the 40–44 and 45–49 age groups amongst rural women was also higher than that for the national population. A comparison of the age patterns of use of pregnancy terminations amongst rural black women for 1997–8 and 2004   reflects much more use of pregnancy terminations amongst the under-20 years, 20–24 and 25–29 age cohorts in 2004 than earlier, while the older age cohorts reflected declining use of the procedure in recent years. This may signify the setting in of lower age normative patterns for the use of pregnancy terminations, which suggests a need to space childbirths.

While the 1998 data indicated that women with zero births were less likely to request pregnancy terminations, a comparison of the 1998 and 2004 data on rural TOPs revealed an increase in rural women who terminated pregnancies at zero childbirth in 2004, thus postponing childbearing. But the largest increase in pregnancy terminations in 2004 followed the first childbirth. After the second childbirth, pregnancy terminations were still much higher amongst rural women in 2004 than in the 1998 scenario. After the third and subsequent childbirths, they remained much lower than in the 1998 rural sample, indicating that pregnancy terminations might be having a bigger demand predominantly for regulating childbirths at lower parities. Overall, pregnancy terminations are requested across all parities amongst rural women, suggesting that other realities than having a child assume major importance for individual rural women at given points in their lives.

The 1994 Programme of Action recommends that pregnancy termination should not replace family planning, but contribute towards reducing the health impact of unsafe abortion. It adds that family planning services should be expanded to reduce recourse to abortion. It is unclear how this important recommendation is addressed in South Africa's reproductive agenda for women.

The context in which pregnancy terminations for rural women are provided warrants some elaboration. South Africa's innovative strategy of training midwives to provide the service, in the face of inadequate medical personnel, has been commended (Dickson-Tetteh and Billings 2002). The supportive contribution several NGOs played in building the requisite competencies amongst health care providers throughout the country to meet the new challenge and the barriers that had to be faced was also commended. It was, however, observed that abortion services benefited urban women disproportionately, leaving the rural women exposed to the risks of unsafe abortions, thus recreating the scenario which prompted the Termination of Pregnancy Act in the first place. Limited support for pregnancy termination services was identified as a barrier in rural KwaZulu-Natal amongst both communities and nurses, except for cases of rape, incest and where continued pregnancy would endanger the woman's health (Harrison *et al.* 2000). Similar reactions were found in the predominantly rural Limpopo province, where intimidation and gun violence threats to TOP providers were made, along with derogatory labels such as "Bin-Laden", "Lucifer" and "Pharaoh" (Mitchell *et al.* 2005). The reality of rural women's demand for pregnancy terminations must be understood against these individual and group aversions to the procedure.

Three of the six rural hospitals from which the 2004 data was collected for this research did not provide TOP services, and those that did had a large influx of local as well as referred clients that requested the service, indicating its high demand. In addition, many clients whose names appeared on the TOP records were turned away from the services because their pregnancies exceeded the permissible pregnancy duration for the procedure, suggesting that the prescribed regulation of the procedure has yet to be fully grasped by rural women, to improve its accessibility to them. Pregnancy durations were also extended because lengthy searches for centres which provide the service, with delays, social and financial hardships for women and their families (Mitchell *et a.* 2005). A report that was posted on the internet by the North-West Provincial Health Department (Gaoganediwe 2004) on the other hand decries the persistent abandoning of newborn babies and back-street abortions, despite the existence of 13 pregnancy termination sites in that province with trained service providers. The inadequacy of the services against a background of high teenage pregnancies was acknowledged in the report, but attention was also drawn to the need for intensified sexuality and peer education work amongst teenagers.

The alleged failure to use existing pregnancy termination services might suggest accessibility problems and attitudinal barriers, financial and other constraints that warrant investigation and addressing. Many women are apparently still compelled to resort to unsafe pregnancy termination procedures as a result of the uneven distribution of services, shortage of services and ineffective access to services, according to an analysis conducted by Risi and Hulton (2002, 5). However, in evaluating percentages of functioning TOP service sites in South Africa's nine provinces, the Health Systems Trust (2003) reported high percentages of functioning sites designated for TOP services in 2003 in all provinces. This, however, does not rule out the possibilities of uneven distribution and ineffective access as well as other problems that research might identify. The extent of the problems cited by North West Province in other provinces is unknown.

5.2 Rural Women's Perspectives on the Observed Changes in Reproductive Patterns

From the perspective of the focus group discussants (Mfono 2002), the changes in the patterns of reproductive behaviour identified through the quantitative analysis contribute to the improved wellbeing of women, as well as that of their families, and therefore have their unequivocal endorsement. Such changes must therefore be viewed as prompted deliberately and purposefully, and directed at achieving identifiable ends. These ends are mainly the economic wellbeing of households, women's health, beauty and emotional wellbeing. The overall changes in patterns of childbearing have accelerated during the 17-year period considered in this research. While the changes cannot be attributed solely to reproductive health service provision, the role played by the services in facilitating rural women's rational control over their reproductive role, improving their health and productive capacity, and placing women at the disposal of their communities for participation in education, skills training and various developmental undertakings is clear. This scenario is not, however, without some shortfalls. Adolescent reproductive problems remain a source of concern to parents, educators, and developers in general. Developing adolescent-friendly reproductive health approaches remains elusive, not only to the rural populations of South Africa but also to wider South African society as well. Incentives for adolescent postponement of childbearing appear to be warranted.

From the focus group discussions, it emerged that while marriage is viewed as the ideal locus for childbearing and social pressure on married women to reproduce is powerful, unmarried women are drawn into the fringes of this pressure as they advance into mature age and their prospects of entering marital unions progressively recede. The source of such pressure on single women was, however, unclear. The term "pressure" used in this context is comparable to "power" in Foucault's (1978) discussion of the history of sexuality. The underlying rationale of pressure appears to be the value of children in their own right and separately from marriage, the perception of childlessness as unnatural, and of children as providers of emotional benefits and help to women. This can be viewed as a repudiation of both the African patriarchal and colonial traditions of childbearing, in which children were defined by patrilineage within a patriarchal system. Women in the context described here appear to have retained their reproductive identity but shifted some of its aspects outside the frame of both missionary tutoring on sexual expression and reproduction and male rights to the progeny. They have done this despite their precarious economic situation within a patriarchal context, inadvertently pushing their society to re-evaluate its gendered economic imperatives.

The perceived social expectation that women should produce children appears to have been so internalized that it confers a group identity to women. In support of this, one focus group participant inquired, "How can one have no child?"—suggesting that a deliberate choice of childlessness for a woman is absurd. The emotional overtones of childlessness were highlighted by the participants, along with the universality of childbearing among women as the hallmarks of reproductive behaviour that cannot be challenged. What is being challenged by change in the participants' views is the requirement of many children, and even one child dissipates the emotional pressure on the woman to reproduce. The participants indicated that a woman with many children no longer enjoys the unqualified prestige traditionally associated with such an achievement, because of the health and economic risks considered inherent in such reproduction.

Whether the participants' arguments on the value of children to parents are borne out by reality is worth considering. This scenario implies that childbearing among women has largely remained universal despite the decline in the incidence of marriage; implicitly endorsing extra-marital reproduction and defeating the quest of reducing sexual adventurism amongst men since women generally outnumber men during adult years. The traditional societal demands for women's childbearing had clearly defined societal benefits in contexts where children were economic assets, and the clan survival that male offspring ensured had benefits to families in the long run. These social networks and their functions have, however, largely atrophied, leaving behind contexts where the surviving demand for children does not appear to have sound rational grounds. The decline in the number of childbirths must therefore be seen in the light of women's desire for children that is informed largely by emotional needs, hence the acceptance of smaller numbers of children by families.

While all the focus group discussion participants were favourably disposed towards fertility regulation, TOP was not a favoured approach. In interpreting the reactions of the focus group participants, however, one has to realize the constraint imposed by the tendency amongst them to avoid taking positions that are known to have strong social disapproval. All the groups thus attacked TOP with emotional gusto, and no defence for it came forth despite the fact that quantitative data showed that the service enjoys substantial patronage among women across age groups. The argument used in their rejection of TOP is that children are a gift from God, and that abortion is killing an innocent child. What came out clearly from the discussions was that women who decide to terminate pregnancies go though intense emotional turmoil emanating from an internalized value of life that is challenged by TOP.

5.3 A Fertility Transition Perspective on the Findings of this Analysis

Because the African fertility transition is appearing after analysts have examined the dynamics of the phenomenon as it occurred in Europe, and has advanced in several Asian countries in recent years, comparing its dynamics with those of these earlier contexts might be enlightening on its likely future course. Thus Caldwell, Orobuloye and Caldwell (1992) announced, on the basis of their observation of changing reproductive patterns in a number of African countries, that the emerging fertility transition has a uniquely distinctive pattern. They based their argument on observations of differences between the societies compared in constraints on premarital sexual behaviour, marital stability and birth spacing, noting in particular the strong proscriptions of female premarital sexual involvement and contraceptive access in Asian societies, which suggest minimal pre-marital regulation of childbirths. Their argument is, however, based on marital patterns, rather than on age patterns of contraception. This leaves their conclusion that postponement of childbirths in Asian societies does not play a significant role in the change to lower birth rates open to question, since childbirth postponement within marriage remains an open course in those contexts. Caldwell, Orobuloye, and Caldwell (1992) also noted that analyses of fertility transition in Europe make no reference to significant postponement of onset of childbearing as a contributing factor, but instead highlight the patterns of limiting childbirth within marital unions.

Caldwell, Orobuloye, and Caldwell (1992) point to a demand for contraception amongst young women in their research on the selected African populations that arises from wishes to postpone childbearing to accommodate education, secure employment and ultimately enter into marriage. Occurrence of early pregnancies upsets this desired progression, forcing women into coerced marriages. Despite governmental efforts to constrain adolescent access to contraception as a measure of controlling their sexual involvement, demographic and health surveys indicate that contraception in the societies in question is more widespread among never-married women than among currently married women. This is reinforced by a high incidence of abortions as unmarried women battle to delay childbearing, in order to maintain their desired sequence of priorities in place. They also note that contraception by African women is also used to substitute for post-partum and terminal sexual abstinence. Observing this scenario, Caldwell and colleagues conclude that the African fertility transition will be characterized by a similarity in the decline of childbirths across all reproductive age groups. The demand for contraception they envisage will simultaneously arise from women wanting to postpone childbearing, those who need to space births and those who need to limit the number of births. They also suggested that in the context of structural adjustment programmes, economic considerations would also prompt behavioural changes aimed at limiting births. The pattern of fertility decline they described was observed from comparisons of consecutive Demographic and Health Survey findings in Zimbabwe, Kenya, Botswana and Senegal.

In their evaluation of the South African fertility decline, however, Caldwell and Caldwell (1993) argued that the transition pattern indicated by their findings was not consistent with the African pattern. Their evaluation was based on previous research evidence, which indicated an apparent low demand for contraception by women under 25 years, and a growing demand for contraception with advancing age. Constrained access to contraception for the younger age cohorts in South Africa created a picture of low demand for contraception from these age groups. When contraception was made accessible to women of all reproductive ages in accordance with the recommendations set out in the Programme of Action, as indicated in Table 4.5., the demand was modest amongst adolescents but the highest in the 20–24 and 25–29 age cohorts. The South African contraceptive use scenario has been changing and inclining towards the African scenario described by Caldwell and colleagues (1992). The unfolding contraceptive use scenario might be similarly driven by women's educational aspirations.

In the populations considered in this research, however, the median age at childbearing was much higher than it was in the societies included in Caldwell, Orobuloye, Caldwell's (1992) analysis. But the South African pattern of reproductive change is apparently dominated by spacing of childbirths, especially the spacing of second births, and child spacing by contraception was reinforced by pregnancy terminations, whose intensity after first childbirths is high. The contribution of non-marital childbearing to fertility transition in the subject population is also worth highlighting. Discussions of the erstwhile European fertility transition make reference to an insignificant incidence of non-marital childbearing that was of no consequence to the overall fertility trends (Knodel and Van de Walle 1986). Analyses of fertility transitions in Asia make no reference to non-marital childbearing. In the context considered in this research, the incidence of non-marital childbearing was high, and was accompanied by fewer births, causing a downward pull on overall fertility.

Marital incidence has relevance to these contexts. Coale (1986) estimated that in pre-transition western European societies, late marriage and women who did not enter marital unions reduced childbirths by up to 50 per cent of its potential level, if all women of ages 15–50 years were married. The societies cited in the African fertility transition theory, on the other hand, have a high incidence of marriage, and Caldwell Orobuloye, and Caldwell (1993) point out that girls who become pregnant are coerced into marriage. Conversely, in the South African context, Udjo (1996) estimated that late marriage and the low marital incidence amongst blacks in South Africa reduced birth rates by 27 per cent of its potential level. The late age at childbearing onset, late marriage and non-marital childbearing combine to set the South African black population apart from the postulated African fertility transition because of the accelerative momentum they add to the transition process, despite similar contraceptive use patterns. The childbearing progression of the subject population was also very distinctive in the wide spacing of lower order births. All these aspects give the South African black rural women's childbearing scenario a tenuous resemblance to the purported African transition to lower childbirths.

5.4 Non-Marital Childbearing and its Implications in the Subject Populations

Non-marital childbearing is one of the prominent characteristics revealed by the statistical data of the emerging reproductive behaviour of the populations under consideration. The samples on childbearing that were drawn for this research were reflected in Chapter 3, and showed the approximate marital status composition of childbearing women at each of the time periods of the research. Budlender, Chobokoane and Simelane's analysis (2004) of the marital status of black South African women established that by the age of 50 years and above, the ever married percentage of black women was 80.4 per cent. The singulate mean ages at marriage (SMAM) for black women estimated from the 1995 and 1999 October Household Surveys and the 1996 Census were all above 30 years. This suggests late marriage, and when considered against the reproductive scenarios that emerged from the data analysis, suggests considerable premarital reproduction.

Women who reported themselves as unmarried constituted 25, 46 and 60 per cent of the samples drawn during 1987–89, 1998 and 2004 years of this research. In the Victoria East District, Mfono (2002) found that the percentage of women who reported their current marital status as single increased from 52 per cent in the 1988 sample to 69 per cent in the 1998 sample. With the protracted nature of forming marital unions in the populations considered, which means that childbearing often precedes the formalization of marriages, it must be conceded that the incidence of non-marital childbearing is high.

The focus group discussion participants (Mfono 2002) acknowledged that non-marital childbearing is not the most acceptable option in their communities. It is, however, tolerated and in fact encouraged when a woman fails to enter into a marital union by a certain undefined mature age, especially if she has the economic wherewithal to support the children born. By and large, the participants perceived non-marital childbearing as a better option compared to childlessness. Does the position postulated by the focus group discussants hold credibility? Non-marital childbearing is after all strongly condemned by many societies and challenges Christian moral principles to which the societies whose reproductive patterns are subjected to scrutiny subscribe.

Burman and Preston-Whyte (1992) express the view that non-marital childbearing in the African societies of South Africa was unwelcome even before the influence of Christianity on African attitudes, a view which suggests that non-marital childbearing is contrary to the traditions of the subject populations. They, however, note that the nature of the stigma associated with non-marital childbearing was determined by different concerns to those imported with Christianity, namely that the girl's family suffered economic loss as a result of the fall in her bride-wealth. Women's attitudes on the matter of bride-wealth as the determinant of who their reproductive partner should be is noted to have shifted dramatically over the years. The traditional songs with lyrics which heaped scorn on the man who could not pay bride-wealth have disappeared. They have been replaced by lyrical content which puts women's feelings towards the favoured man above his capacity to reward the woman's interest in him with bride wealth payments[2]. In addition; the favoured man may be married. Within the prevailing context of monogamy, the prospect of marriage for the woman involved in the relationship may not be on the cards, non-marital childbearing being the only course that is open.

Women's sexual and reproductive actions have thus come to be based largely on their personal emotional attachments, and not on the pragmatism and economic convenience for their families, as prescribed by the traditional system. The economic loss suffered by the girl's family from non-marital childbearing has thus deepened over the years, because it arises from both the loss of the bride-wealth that is due to the girl's family in traditional terms, as well as from the imposition of the economic liability of having to maintain the girl's child or children, if the biological father is incapable or unwilling to do so. In addition, non-marital childbearing in a context of social change raises questions of filiations and clan identity of the non-marital offspring, along with confrontations between custom and tradition on child maintenance and legitimate guardianship of the affected children if their mother should get married to someone other than the biological father.

Non-marital childbearing by a considerable proportion of women in the population considered in this research, despite accessible contraception, might be regarded as a conscious choice. Women who make such a choice have been described by Preston-Whyte (1992) as having "a jaundiced" view of marriage. Viewed in this way, non-marital childbearing provides yet another rationale for gender egalitarian policies in aspects like inheritance, access to land, human resource development and economic opportunities. Strategies that enhance women's capacity to raise children are a realistic course of action from a perspective of social justice.

---

[2] In the 1970s, a popular musical group, the Mahotella Queens hit the South African radio stations with a song about their chosen lover, Dlamini. The lyrics of this Zulu song can be translated thus: "Dlamini, I love him, I love him, I love him. He may not have cattle or money. I don't care, I love him, I love him, I love him." Songs with similar lyrical content were to follow this one, indicating the assertiveness of girls against gerontocratic coercion into unions based on men's capacity to pay bride-wealth.

5.5 AIDS and Rural Women's Reproductive Patterns in the Research Context

A discussion of a reproductive scenario in South Africa would be incomplete without considering the impact of AIDS on reproduction, which has been spreading at an accelerated pace in the subject populations as well as the wider population of South Africa. AIDS education focuses on sexual norms in its insistence on sexual abstinence and use of condoms, both of which eventually impact on the incidence of conceptions and childbirths. The rising age at childbearing onset in the subject populations, particularly in KwaZulu-Natal, as well as the growth in proportions of women with zero childbirths might be the outcomes of concerted emphases on sexual abstinence amongst young people. These developments, however, require more intensive analysis of their dynamics than what has been covered in the present study.

AIDS affects all aspects of life in South Africa, especially amongst women, who are bearing the brunt of higher infection rates than men. The spread of AIDS indicates that the prescriptions on healthier sexual normative behaviour do not generate the requisite behavioural responses. More importantly from the point of view of this research, protection against AIDS through sexual abstinence and condom use might be having reproductive outcomes, as well as health and human rights outcomes that are not acknowledged in the findings of this research, which relies on records data. AIDS infections also destroy the childbearing aspirations of couples by attacking their physical capacity to reproduce, but these factors are difficult to quantify.

Some qualitative information based on focus group discussions (Mfono 2002) indicates women's perceptions of the reproductive health scenario confronting them in the face of AIDS. While women concede that they gained some control over their childbearing because of the accessibility of various family planning methods, their control over their sexual relations with their partners is limited and mostly dependent on their partners' co-operation. This situation apparently prevails both in marital and non-marital sexual relations. The research participants noted that suggesting condom use to a sexual partner elicited accusations of the woman's unfaithfulness to the relationship. Male partners were depicted as always jealous and suspicious about women's loyalty in relationships, while male partners in turn engaged in endless sexual exploits. While discussants appeared to have largely accepted the unfaithfulness of their partners, the discussions revealed their intense concerns about the implications of the widespread unfaithfulness in the face of AIDS.

The AIDS scenario simultaneously raises questions of women's rights to bodily integrity as set out in the South African constitution, as well as husbands' cultural prerogative to the deployment of sexual privileges by their wives as prescribed by the lobola custom. In addition to these considerations, the Programme of Action incorporated AIDS prevention strategies, which overlap with those recommended by health workers. The AIDS scenario generally has a deleterious effect on women's reproductive choices.

5.6 Summary of the Findings Discussed in this Work

The analysis found that rural women reflect an upward trend in ages at onset and progression of childbearing as well as progressive declines in the mean number of childbirths. Wide spacing of lower order births might increase the incidence of late childbearing in future years. Child-spacing is playing a prominent role in the observed changes, and is facilitated by the accessibility of reproductive health service technology.

The decline in childbirths that has been noted by major surveys in South Africa extends to the black rural communities encompassed in this research and is gaining momentum. Childbearing amongst women in the rural populations considered is universal and largely unconstrained by the declining incidence of marriage or the increase in marital age. Women presumably view childbearing as a requirement for social acceptance, but for married women it is seen as obligatory as prescribed by tradition. However, fewer children per woman are becoming normative, with unmarried women having fewer children than married women. Economic, health and beauty considerations are behind these trends.

The decline in births in the population considered follows the African pattern in which postponement, spacing and limiting of births have each a significant role in the decline of the incidence of childbirths. The marital patterns of the subject population, however, gave an accelerative momentum to the fall in birth rates. Also childbearing onset was late, when compared to what it is in the posited African transition context. Economic considerations and the growing desirability of unhampered school participation also prompted negative attitudes towards early childbearing by girls engaged in formal education. Adolescent contraception, however, still leaves much to be desired, despite the median age of 20 years at onset of childbearing.

The incidence of non-marital childbearing in the population considered was higher than that of marital childbearing at the lower order births, particularly at first childbirths. Marital and non-marital childbearing showed different patterns, with non-marital childbearing having an earlier mean age of onset but a smaller number of childbirths. Its predominance means that it determines the overall pattern of lower total childbirths. This is an unusual scenario for an African society, and finds an unequivocal African parallel in Botswana, but also possibly in some Latin American and Caribbean societies.

The emerging age and parity pattern of use of pregnancy terminations amongst rural women showed a close resemblance to that of contraceptive use, being dominated by the younger age cohorts, and concentrated amongst women with one previous childbirth. The result indicated that the ages at which rural women request sterilization are dropping, but parity patterns yet had a directional trend. All the changes in reproductive patterns observed are, however, gradual compared to the national trends for black women even though the gaps are narrowing.

Women in the population considered appeared to have achieved a considerable control over their childbearing with the availability of female methods of contraception, sterilization, and pregnancy termination services. The latter services command substantial patronage, despite the expressed reservations about them raised by participants in the focus group discussions. However, participants also revealed that control over sexual relations resides with male partners, and this deprives women of any role in controlling the spread of AIDS.

Where provincial trends are concerned, the rural Eastern Cape Province appeared to lag behind the other four provinces compared in many of the changes that are taking place in rural women's reproductive patterns. Except for pregnancy terminations, which depended a lot on referrals, reproductive health services appear to provide rural women with reasonable reproductive health choices even though there are indications of regional disparities in accessibility of services within provinces.

As childbirths are falling progressively amongst rural women, and as the women remain strong and healthy, the need for alternative and meaningful direction of rural women's energies to development undertakings has to be heeded. Otherwise, rural women might constitute an under-utilized human resource.

5.7 Policy and Further Research Recommendations from the Findings

The following policy recommendations emerged from the findings of this research.

- As noted above, the 1994 Programme of Action made reference to the involvement of men in the implementation of its recommendations on women's reproductive changes that empower them for involvement in development. Without men crafting their role in relation to the Programme of Action and becoming facilitators of the processes of development and change that confront their societies, achievements are likely to be protracted. Policies are, however, unlikely to go beyond specifying individual rights on bodily integrity and reproductive choices for everyone, as the South African constitution does. The details of harmonious reproductive partnerships that accommodate women's reproductive changes must ultimately be negotiated between the reproductive partners and compromises be reached on reconciling traditionally prescribed aspects like payment of bride-wealth and childbirths. It remains the government's responsibility to make men broadly aware of the challenging tasks placed at their doorstep, and to provide platforms for men to interrogate the tasks allocated to them and arrive at strategies of addressing themselves to them.

- Non-marital childbearing of the scale observed in the subject populations calls for policies that recognize the growing incidence of female household heads, and addressing it through economic and social justice that ensures women's unreserved participation in political, social and economic developmental undertakings, to enhance their capacity to sustain their households in accordance with their capacities. While the constitution of South Africa provides for gender equality, the evolving of such equality requires diligent monitoring. Households headed by women need not be poor in a socially just society.

- The question of adolescent access to contraception remains an issue that warrants both research as well as research-based policy interventions. As with the provision of school nutrition programmes, mobile clinic services with a strong sexuality education component for high schools pupils might be of great benefit to this group. The increase between 1998 and 2004 of adolescents who used pregnancy terminations to postpone childbirth can be taken as an indication that many adolescent pregnancies occur unintentionally, and that there might still be serious problems concerning adolescent access to contraception, including attitudinal barriers that require creative interventions.

- Children's grants have been criticized as providing incentives for adolescent childbirths. Probably the situation could be turned around such that girls who complete their adolescent years without any childbirth receive free tertiary level education for a delimited number of years. In this way, an incentive for postponing childbirth would be created, and the developmental options of the affected women would be vastly expanded.

- In deference to South African individuals and groups that find TOP objectionable, and also in recognition to TOP's demand to women, the government might consider a policy of regular monitoring of accessibility of the other methods of regulating childbirths and making the findings of such accessibility public in order to ensure responsible use of TOP services. Sub-provincial, regional and sub-regional monitoring of reproductive health accessibility could indicate priority intervention areas. In this regard, women might also be swayed away persuasively from using TOP as a family planning measure, but as a means of last resort. Such monitoring might heighten governmental and public commitment to ensuring accessibility of the less controversial family planning methods, as well as generate active support from the irate TOP opponents.

- Rural reproductive changes could be accompanied by governmental programmes that meaningfully engage rural women's time that is being released from chores associated with childbearing. Participation in local projects, adult education, and skills training are some of the developmental options which could be made readily available to rural women.

- Women's reproductive behaviour patterns might benefit from being subsumed under gender policy, because of their high women's rights, women's health, and women's development content and the considerable potential for synergy for gender policy and strategies addressing women's reproductive needs.

Based on the findings, the following were indicated as areas of further research.

- The existence of sub-provincial disparities in rural women's access to reproductive health services, as highlighted in one of the provinces in this research calls for further sub-provincial analyses to identify similar sub-provincial scenarios. Such areas need to be treated as priority intervention areas in the provision of reproductive health services.

- Non-marital childbearing is one of the hallmarks of the subject populations. While its economic and demographic implications have been subjected to analyses, its dynamics and social implications for the societies affected is a neglected area from a research perspective.

- One of the five provinces included in this research, KwaZulu-Natal, reflected the highest ages at onset of childbearing but low use of contraception, suggesting much lower levels of adolescent exposure to conception. More research of this scenario and its dynamics might generate information on approaches that could benefit other rural provincial populations in their quest for managing adolescent reproductive patterns.

- Theoretical analyses of fertility transition should recognize and pay attention to non-marital childbearing and its distinctive features.

REFERENCES

Abercrombie, N., S. Hill, and B. S. Turner. 1984. *The dominant ideology thesis.* London: George Allen and Unwin.

Armstrong, A.K., C. Beyani, C. Himonga, J. Kabeberi-Macharia *et al.* 1993. Uncovering reality: Excavating women's rights in African family law. *International Journal of Law and Family* 7: 314–369.

Ba, M. 1980. *So long a letter.* Oxford: Heinemann.

Backhouse, J. 1844. *A narrative of a visit to Mauritius and South Africa.* London: Hamilton Adams.

Bility, K. 1996.   What South African children think about reproductive health. *Sexual and Reproductive Health Bulletin, no.3* (September): 6–7.

Bongaarts, J. 1983. *Fertility, biology and behaviour: An analysis of the proximate fertility determinants.* New York: Academic Press.

Bozzoli, B. and M. Nkotsoe. 1991. *Women in Phokeng.* Johannesburg: Ravan Press.

Budlender, D., N. Chobokoane and S Simelane. 2004. Marriage patterns in South Africa: Methodological and substantive issues. *Southern African Journal of Demography* 9, 1 (June): 1–25.

Burch, T.K. 1983. The impact of forms of families and sexual unions and dissolution of unions on fertility. In *Determinants of fertility in developing countries,* edited by R. A. Bulatao and R.D. Lee, Vol. 2, 532–561. New York: Academic Press.

Burman, S. 1990. Fighting a two-pronged attack: The changing legal status of women in Cape-ruled Basutoland, 1872–1884. In *Women and gender in Southern Africa to 1945,* edited by C. Walker, 48–75. Cape Town: David Philip.

_____ 1991. Illegitimacy and the African family in a changing South Africa. In *Acta Juridica,* 36–51. Cape Town: Juta & Co. Ltd.

Burman, S. and E. Preston-Whyte. 1992. Assessing illegitimacy in South Africa. In *Questionable issue: Illegitimacy in South Africa,* edited by S. Burman and E. Preston-Whyte. Cape Town: Oxford University Press.

Caldwell, J.C. 1982. *Theory of fertility decline.* London: Academic Press.

Caldwell, J.C., I.O. Orobuloye and P. Caldwell. 1992. Fertility decline in Africa: A new type of transition? *Population and Development Review* 18, 2: 211–243.

Caldwell, J.C. and P. Caldwell. 1987. The cultural context of high fertility in sub-Saharan Africa. *Population and Development Review* 13, 3: 409–437.

_____ 1993. The South African fertility decline. *Population and Development Review* 19, 2 (June): 225–261.

Clark, B. and B. van Heerden. 1992. The legal position of children born out of wedlock. In *Questionable issue: Illegitimacy in South Africa*, edited by S. Burman and E. Preston-Whyte, 36–63. Cape Town: Oxford University Press.

Cleland, J. and C. Wilson. 1987. Demand theories of the fertility transition: An iconoclastic view. *Population Studies* 41:5–30.

Cleland, J. and M. M. Ali. 2004. Reproductive consequences of contraceptive failure in developing countries. *Obstetrics and Gynecology,* 104, 2 (August): 314–20.

Coale, A.J. 1986. The decline of fertility in Europe since the eighteenth century as a chapter in demographic history. In *The decline of fertility in Europe,* edited by A. J. Coale and S.C. Watkins, 1–30. New Jersey: Princeton.

Coale, A. J and S.C. Watkins (eds). 1986. *The decline of fertility in Europe.* New Jersey: Princeton.

David, H.P. 1983. Abortion: Its prevalence correlates and costs. *In Determinants of fertility in developing countries,* edited by . R. A. Bulatao and R.D. Lee, Vol.2, 193–244. New York: Academic Press.

Department of Health, Medical Research Council and Macro International. 1998. South Africa demographic and health survey, Preliminary report. Pretoria: Government Printer.

Department of Welfare. 1998. *Population policy for South Africa. Pretoria:* Ministry of Welfare and Population Development.

Development Bank of Southern Africa.1994. *South Africa's nine provinces: A human development profile.* Halfway House: Development Bank of Southern Africa.

Dickson-Tetteh, K. and D. L. Billings. 2002. Abortion Care Services provided by registered midwives in South Africa. *International Family Planning Perspectives,* 28(3): 144–150. Available <u>online</u> (last accessed 9 February 2005).

Donaldson, L. 1991. *Fertility transition. The social dynamics of population change.* Cambridge: Basil Blackwell.

Du Plessis, G. 1999. Transition in fertility preferences in South Africa: Issues of conscious choice and numeracy. International Population Conference on African Population in the 21st Century,Vol.1, pp.167–191. Dakar: Union of African Population Studies.

Emecheta, B. 1979. *The joys of motherhood.* London: Heinemann.

Ethelston, S., A. Bechtel, N. Chaya, A. Kantner, and C.B. Vogel. 2004. *Progress and promises. Trends in international assistance for reproductive health and population.* Washington: Population Action International.

Foucault, M. 1978. *The History of sexuality*. (Translated from French by Robert Hurley). Hammondsworth: Penguin Books Ltd.

Freedman, L.P. and S. L. Isaacs. 1993. Human rights and reproductive choice. *Studies in Family Planning* 24, 1(January/February): pp.18–30.

Freire, P. 1993. *The pedagogy of the oppressed*. London: Penguin Books.

Fuze, M.M. 1979. *The black people and from whence they came*. (Translated by Campbell, K., Africana Library). Pietermaritzburg: University of Natal Press.

Gaoganediwe, B. 2004. North West health concern with spate of abandoned new-borns. Media Release 27 October, 2004. www.info.gov.za/speeches, Downloaded 10 June 2005.

Garenne, M., S. Tollman and K. Kahn. 2000. Premarital fertility in rural South Africa: A challenge to existing population policy. *Studies in Family Planning* 31, no.1: 47–54.

Glenn, N. D. 1977. *Cohort analysis*. Beverly Hills: Sage Publications.

Gordon, L. 1977. *Woman's body, woman's right: A Social history of birth control in America*. London: Penguin Books.

Gulbrandsen, O. 1986. To marry, or not to marry? Marital strategies and sexual relations in Tswana society. *Ethnos* 51, 1–2: 7–28.

Guy, J. 1990. Gender oppression in Southern Africa's pre-capitalist societies. In *Women and Gender in Southern Africa to 1945*, edited by C. Walker. Cape Town: David Philip.

Handwerker, W.P. 1989. *Women's power and social revolution: Fertility transition in the West Indies*. London: Sage Publications.

Harrison, A., E.T. Montgomery, M. Lurie, and D. Wilkinson. 2000. *Barriers to implementing South African termination of pregnancy in rural KwaZulu-Natal*. Durban: Centre for Epidemiological Research in South Africa.

Hartmann, B. 1995. *Reproductive rights and wrongs*. Boston: South End Press.

Head, B. 1984. *A bewitched crossroad*. AD Donker: Craighall.

Health Systems Trust. 2003. *Health statistics*. http://www.hst.org.za/heathstats/151/data. Last accessed 1/18/2006.

Henry, L., 1961. Some data on natural fertility. *Eugenics Quarterly* 8:81–91.

Hooks, B. 1981. *Ain't I a woman? Black women and feminism*. London: Pluto Press.

Houghton, H. 1956. *The Tomlinson report: A Summary of the findings and recommendations in the Tomlinson Commissiont*. Johannesburg: South African Institute of Race Relations.

Human Sciences Research Council (HSRC). 1987. *The South African demographic and health survey.* Pretoria: HSRC.

Hunter, M. 1936. *Reaction to conquest.* London: Oxford University Press.

Hutchison, P., J. T. Boerma and M. Khan. 2004. 1998 Demographic and health survey for the Eastern Cape Province. Equity Project. Available from: www.cpc.unc.edu/measure/publications

International Federation of Women Lawyers (Kenya Chapter). 1997. *Women of the world: Laws and policies affecting their reproductive lives.* New York: Center for Reproductive Law and Policy.

Johnson, S. 1995. *The Politics of population: Cairo 1994.* London: Earthscan Publications.

Jones, S. 1992. Children on the move: Parenting, mobility and birth status. In *Questionable Issue: Illegitimacy in South Africa,* edited by S. Burman and E. Preston-Whyte`247–278. Cape Town: Oxford University Press.

Jordaan, A.C. 1980. *The wrath of the ancestors.* Alice: Lovedale Press.

Karanja, W.W. 1994. The phenomenon of 'outside wives': Some reflections on its possible influence on fertility. In *Nuptiality in Sub-Saharan Africa,* edited by C. Bledsoe and G. Pison, 194–214. Oxford: Clarendon Press.

Karim, Q.A., S.A. Karim and J. Nkomokazi. 1991. Sexual behaviour and knowledge of AIDS among black urban mothers: Implications for AIDS intervention programmes. *South African Medical Journal 80*: 340–343.

Kaufman, C.E, T. de Wet, and J. Stadler. 2000. Adolescent parenthood and subsequent fertility in South Africa. *Studies in Family Planning,* 32(2), 147–160.

Knodel J. and E. De dan Walle. 1986. Lessons from the past: Policy implications of historical fertility studies. In *The decline of fertility in Europe,* edited by A.J. Coale and S.C. Watkins, 391–441. Princeton: Princeton University Press.

Krige, E. J. 1936. Changing conditions in marital relations and parental duties among urbanised natives. *Africa,* 9: 405–430.

Lesthaeghe, R. 1983. A century of demographic and cultural change in Western Europe: An exploration of underlying dimensions. *Population and Development Review* 9, 3 (September): 411–435.

LeVine, R.A. and C.M. Scrimshaw. 1983. Effects of culture on fertility: Anthropological contributions. In *Determinants of fertility in developing countries,* edited by R. A. Bulatao and R.D. Lee, Vol. 2, 666–695. New York: Academic Press.

Malthus, T.R. 1992. *An essay on the principle of population.* Cambridge: Cambridge University Press.

Mandela, N. R. 1994. *Long walk to freedom.* Johannesburg: McDonald.

Martin, T. C. 1997. Marriages without Papers in Latin America. *International Population Conference, Beijing.* Vol. 2. Liege: International Union for Scientific Study of Population. 941–960.

Mayer, P. 1980. The origin and decline of two rural resistance ideologies. In *Black villagers in an industrial society,* edited by P. Mayer, 1–89. Cape Town: Oxford University Press.

Mayer, P. and I. Mayer. 1974. *Townsmen or tribesmen: Conservatism and the process of urbanization in a South African city.* Cape Town: Oxford University Press.

Mencarini, L. 1999. An analysis of fertility and infant mortality in South Africa based on LSDS data. *The African population in the 21st Century.* Vol.1. 109–127. Dakar: Union of African Population Studies.

Mfono, Z.N. 1999. Teenage contraceptive needs in urban South Africa: A case study. *International Family Planning Perspectives* 24, 4 (December): 180–183.

______ 2002. An analysis of the emerging patterns of reproductive behaviour among rural women: A case study of the Victoria East district of the Eastern Cape Province. Unpublished PhD Thesis. Stellenbosch: University of Stellenbosch.

Mill, J.S. 1909. *Principles of political economy.* Vol.1. New York: Appleton.

______. 1929. Two speeches on population. *The Journal of Adult Education,* Vol. 4, October 1929.

Mishra, S. 1983. Poignant problems, *People,* (IPPF), 10, no.4: 7-9.

Mitchell, E., M. H. Kelvin, M. Mwaba, M. Sophie, and T. Karen. 2005. *A facility assessment of termination of pregnancy (TOP) services in Limpopo Province, South Africa.* Chapel Hill, NC, Ipas. Available online (last accessed 9 February 2005).

Molokomme, A. 1996. State intervention in the family: A case study of the child maintenance law in Botswana. In *Shifting circles of support: Contextualizing gender and kinship in South Asia and Sub-Saharan Africa,* edited by R. Palriwala and C. Risseeu, 270–301. London: Alata Mira Press.

Mphahlele, E. 1979. *Chirundu.* Johannesburg: Ravan Press.

Ngubane, H.N. 1977. *Body and mind in Zulu medicine.* Academic Press: London.

Nhlapo, T. 1991. Women's rights and the family in traditional and customary law. In *Putting women on the agenda,* edited by S. Bozolli, 111–123. Johannesburg: Ravan Press.

Notestein, F.W. 1953. Economic problems and population change. In *Proceedings of the Eighth International Conference of Agricultural Economists.* 13–31. London: Oxford University Press.

Nuruddin, F. 1970. *From a crooked rib.* London: Heinemann.

Oosthuizen, K. 1997. Similarities and differences between the fertility decline in Europe and the emerging decline in sub-Saharan Africa. In Beijing International Population Conference Papers, Vol. 3, 1063–1090, Liege: IUSSP.

Panel on Population Dynamics in Sub-Saharan Africa. 1993. *Demographic change in sub-Saharan Africa.* In Population Dynamics of Sub-Saharan Africa, edited by Foote, K.A. and L.G. Martin. New York: National Academy.

Pauw, B.A. 1975. *Christianity and Xhosa tradition.* Cape Town: Oxford University Press.

Pauw, B, 1976. Bantu social organization. In *Standard Encyclopedia of Southern Africa, Vol.2,* 156–160. Elsies River: National Commercial Printers.

Pearce, F. 2000. The microbe that shaped Africa. *Mail & Guardian,* December 15–21, 2000.

Peteni. R.L. 1976. *Hill of fools.* London: Heinemann.

Population Council. 1995. Programme of Action of the 1994 International Conference on Population and Development (Chapters I-VIII). *Population and Development Review* 21, No.1(March): 187–213.

Potts, D. and S. Marks. 2001. Fertility decline in Southern Africa: The quiet revolution. *Journal of Southern African Studies* 27, no. 2:189–205.

Preston-Whyte, E.M. and M. Zondi. 1992. African teenage pregnancy: Whose problem? In *Questionable Issue: Illegitimacy in South Africa,* edited by S. Burman and E. Preston-Whyte, 226–246. Cape Town: Oxford University Press.

_____ 1988. Families without marriage. In *Social system and tradition in Southern Africa,* edited by Argyle, W.J. and E.M. Preston-Whyte, 55–83. Cape Town: Oxford University Press.

Radcliffe-Brown, A.R. and D Forde. 1965. *Systems of kinship and marriage.* London: Oxford University Press.

Raum, O. and E.J. De Jager. 1972. *Transition and change in a rural community.* Alice: Fort Hare University Press.

Reproductive Research Unit. 1997. Facts on the South African abortion scene. In *Sexual and Reproductive Health Bulletin,* Number 4, September, 1997, 3. Observatory: Planned Parenthood Association of South Africa.

Republic of South Africa. 1996. *The Constitution of the Republic of South Africa.* ISBN Publications.

_____ 1996. *Choice on termination of pregnancy Act* No 92 of 1996. ISBN Publications.

Retherford, R.D. and J.A. Palmore. 1983. Diffusion processes affecting fertility regulation. In *The decline of fertility in Europe*, edited by A. J.Coale and S. C. Watkins, 295–339. Princeton: Princeton University Press.

Risi, L. and L. Hulton. 2002. Increasing access to reproductive health services through social business: The role of Marie Stopes South Africa in delivering termination of pregnancy services. *Working Papers Series*, No.6.

Saadawi, N. 1983. *Woman at point zero*. London: Zed Books.

Schapera, I. 1933. Premarital pregnancy and native opinion: A note on social change. *Africa* 6: 59–89.

______. 1971. *Married life in an African tribe*. London: Pelican.

Smith, P.C. 1983. Age at marriage, proportions marrying and Fertility. In *Determinants of fertility in developing countries*, edited by R. A. Bulatao and R.D. Lee, *Vol.2*, 473–531. New York: Academic Press.

Soga, J.H. 1931. *The Ama-Xosa life and customs*. Alice: Lovedale Press.

South African Department of Health (SADH). 1998. *Demographic and Health Survey 1998*. Pretoria: Distributed by the South African Data Archive, Pretoria.

South African Labour and Development Research Unit. 1993. *Project Statistics on Living Standards and Development (PSLSD)*. Cape Town: SALDRU.

Statistics South Africa. 1995. October Household Survey. Pretoria: Government Printer.

______. 1998. Rural Household Survey. Pretoria: Government Printer.

______2001. Census 2001. Pretoria: Government Printer.

______. 2002. *General Household Survey*. Pretoria: Government Printer.

Tabah, L. 1989. From one demographic transition to another. *Population bulletin of the United Nations*, 28:1–21.

Thomas, H. 1989. *An unfinished history of the world*. London: Pan Books.

Timaeus, I. and W.Graham. 1989. Labor circulation, marriage, and fertility in Southern Africa. In *Reproduction and social organization in sub-Saharan Africa*, edited by R.J. Lesthaeghe, 365–400. Berkeley: University of California Press.

Udjo, E.O. 1996. *Marital patterns and fertility in South Africa: Evidence from the 1996 population census*. Pretoria: Statistics South Africa.

United Nations.1968. *Teheran conference on human rights*. New York: United Nations.

______. 1979. *Convention on elimination of all forms of discrimination against women*. New York: United Nations.

______. 1987. *The world fertility survey*. New York: United Nations.

United Nations Fund for Population Activities. 1997. *Programme review and strategy development report*. Pretoria: UNFPA.

Van der Vliet.V. 1982. Black marriages: Expectations and aspirations in an urban environment. Unpublished Master's Thesis, University of the Witwatersrand.

_____. 1991. Traditional husbands, modern wives? Constructing marriages in a lack African township. In *Tradition and transition in Southern Africa*, edited by A.D. Speigel and A. McAllister, 219–241. Johannesburg: Witwatersrand University Press.

Vaughn, J.H., 1994. African marriage and family. In *Encyclopedia of social history*, edited by P. N. Stears, Vol. 13. New York: Garland Publishing Company.

Whiteford, A., D. Posel and T. Kelatwang. 1995. *A Profile of poverty, inequality and human development*. Pretoria: HSRC.

Wilson, M. 1971. *Religion and transformation of society. A study in social change in Africa*. Cambridge: Cambridge University Press.

_____. 1981. Xhosa marriage in historical perspective. In *Essays on African marriage in Southern Africa*, edited by J.E. Krige and J. L. Comaroff, 133–147. Cape Town: Juta and Company Limited.

Wilson, M. and Thompson, L. (editors) 1969. *The Oxford history of South Africa*, Vol.1. Oxford: Oxford University Press.

Wilson, M., S. Kaplan, T. Maki, and E. M. Walton. 1952. *Social structure, Keiskammahoek rural survey*. Vol.3. Pietermaritzburg: Shuter and Shooter.

World Health Organisation. 1978. Declaration of Alma Ata. www.who.dk/AboutWHO/Policy/20010827_1 (last accessed on 12 June, 2006).

ANNEXURE 1

A SYNOPTIC DESCRIPTION OF THE 1987–89 SOUTH AFRICAN DEMOGRAPHIC AND HEALTH SURVEY

Study Description

SADA 0115

TITLE: Demographic and Health Survey (1987)

Principal Investigators

Human Sciences Research Council (HSRC)

Depositor: Human Sciences Research Council (HSRC)

Abstract: The Demographic and Health Survey is mainly concerned with the determination of fertility, infant mortality rates and closely related issues. Questions surrounding respondent's background, reproduction, contraception, health and breastfeeding, marriage, fertility preferences, and husband's background and woman's work were asked. This study consists of two datasets, one an household dataset and the other an individual dataset, the respondent being a female of reproductive age that has already given birth or who is married or exposed to pregnancy. Females qualifying for the individual interview schedule were chosen from the responses to household (cover) questionnaire.

Geographic Location: South Africa.

Important Variables: Type of dwelling, reproduction, health and breastfeeding, contraception, marriage, fertility preference, husband's background and woman's work amongst others.

Demographic Variables: Standard, general demographic and biographic information such as place of residence, age, educational qualifications, religion and language amongst others.

Universe: Females of reproductive age that have already given birth or who are married or exposed to pregnancy.

Method of Data Collection – Sampling. Random samples of clusters of households, representative of the main lifestyles in every participating state or region were selected.

Fieldwork Agency: Human Sciences Research Council conducted the fieldwork as described in the method of data collection.

Type of Instrument: Structured interview schedule/questionnaire.

Units of Observation: One case/unit equals one person/respondent.

WEIGHTING: No weighting

Date of Data Collection: 1987

Extent of Data Collection: two data files in SPSS and hardcopy documentation and questionnaire.

Main Individual Questionnaire Dataset

Number of cases:	21 842
Number of records:	21 842
Number of records per case:	1
Logical Record Length:	80+
Number of Variables:	100
Number of Kilobytes:	19, 180KB

Household (Cover) Questionnaire Dataset

Number of cases:	14 048
Number of records:	14 048
Number of records per case:	1
Logical Record Length:	80+
Number of Variables:	65
Number of Kilobytes:	2, 287KB

ANNEXURE 2

A SYNOPTIC DESCRIPTION OF THE 1998 SOUTH AFRICAN DEMOGRAPHIC AND HEALTH SURVEY, (SADHS, 1998)

Principal Investigator: Department of Health

The Aim of the Research: A variety of demographic and health indicators were collected in order to achieve the following general objectives:

i.   To continue to the information base for health and population development programme management through accurate and timely data on a range of demographic and health indicators;

ii. To provide baseline data for monitoring programmes and future planning; and

iii. To build research and research management capacity in large-scale national demographic and health surveys.

Demographic Variables: Age, gender, level of education, marital status, use of health services, economic activity, unemployment, employment and self-employment.

Sampling: The sample for the SADHS was designed to be a nationally representative probability sample of approximately 12,000 completed interviews with women between the ages of 15 and 49. The country was stratified into the nine provinces and each province was further stratified into urban and non-urban areas. In addition the Eastern Cape was stratified into five health regions, with each health region stratified into urban and non-urban areas. The sampling frame for the SADHS was the list of approximately 86,000 enumeration areas (EAs) created by the Central Statistical Services, now Statistics South Africa, for the 1996 census. Within each stratum a two-stage sample was selected.

The Primary Sampling Units (PSUs) corresponded to the EAs and were selected with probability proportional to size (pps), the size being the number of census visiting points in the EA. This led to a total of 972 PSUs being selected for the SADHS (690 in urban areas and 282 in non-urban areas). In urban enumeration areas ten households were selected, while in non-urban EAs 20 households were selected. This resulted in a total of 12,860 households being selected throughout the country. Every second household was selected for the adult health survey. In this second household, in addition to interviewing all women aged 15–49, interviewers also interviewed all adults aged 15 and over. It was expected that the sample would yield interviews with approximately 12,000 women aged 15–49 and 13,500 adults.